Passive Income 101 Ways To Earn Passive Income Online

SADANAND PUJARI

Published by SADANAND PUJARI, 2023.

Table of Contents

Copyright 1

About 2

4 Powerful Ways To Earn Passive Income Worldwide! 3

3 More Ways To Earn Passive Income! 10

Step-By-Step Tutorial 14

How Much Does This Pay? 21

4 Apps That Give Money Automatically Once You've Activated 26

3 More Automatic Income Apps 29

1st Way to Make Money While You Are SLEEPING! 32

2nd & 3rd Ways How I Made a Life-Changing PASSIVE Income Online! 35

Most Powerful Way to Earn Passive Income! 38

The FP Model 40

The AA Model 43

The EP Model 46

What to Do RIGHT NOW If You Don't Have Any Money to Invest? 48

The MOST IMPORTANT Investing Video You'll Ever See! 52

Easy Option! 56

UNIQUE Opportunity! 58

What Will Happen NEXT? 61

EYE-OPENING Charts That Will Blow Your Mind! 63

Whats Next 67

Why Should You Aim to Make Passive Income? 69

1 Day Work - 9 Days Rest 72

Do the Work Once & Get Paid for Years to Come! 75

Practical Examples on How to Do This! 78

EASY Ways to Earn Passive Income on This Website 81

MORE Ways to Earn Money on This Website 84

Apps to Get FREE Bitcoin While You're Sleeping 87

MORE Ways to Get Bitcoin Automatically 90

See Step-By-Step How to Earn Money While You Sleep 93

Alternative Ways to Earn Passive Income That I Use Myself . 96

This WORLDWIDE App Pays You FREE Bitcoin DAILY! 99

TRICKS to Earn MORE MONEY with This App! 103

Copyright

Copyright © 2023 by **SADANAND PUJARI**

All rights reserved. No part of this book may be reproduced, scanned, or distributed in any printed or electronic form without permission. Please do not participate in or encourage piracy of copyrighted materials in violation of the author's rights. Purchase only authorized editions.

Passive Income 101 Ways To Earn Passive Income Online

First Edition: Dec 2023

Book Design by **SADANAND PUJARI**

About

If you're someone looking to earn passive income online, this Book is perfect for you. This Book will teach you the ins and outs of creating multiple streams of income and diversifying your services without spending any money upfront.

By the end of this Book, you'll have a thorough understanding of how to add new offerings to your existing business, explore your niche, and create digital products that can help you earn automated income.

This Book is not for those who are not willing to put in the hard work and effort required to create and maintain passive income streams. It is also not for those who are not interested in learning new skills and techniques for earning money online.

Creating passive income takes hard work and dedication, but it is well worth the effort. With the right strategies and techniques, you can enjoy a steady stream of income that will make your life easier and more enjoyable.

Enroll in this Book today to learn how to create, implement, and scale passive income streams!

4 Powerful Ways To Earn Passive Income Worldwide!

I had to take my phone and it told me that I had earned 500 dollar passive income just like that, and actually every single month I receive 500 dollars, 500 dollars, 500 dollars. And this is only one of those seven ways you can make passive income. I'm going to explain exactly how you can make passive income in these seven different ways. All you need to do is just go to what is up your guys. It's right up here. And in this way, from three to seven different ways, how you can make passive income anywhere in the world.

Passive income means that you will make money even while you are sleeping or while you are laying down at the beach enjoying the sunshine or spending time with your loved ones, with your girlfriend or with your kids if you have some kids. So this is something absolutely amazing and very exciting, all excited to create a suite. And I'm sure you will find this valuable. So let's start with number one. This is, in my personal opinion, the easiest way, the easiest way to make money.

We make passive income online. And this is probably the first way I also personally start making some passive income online. And it is called stock market investing. What it basically means is that it is fueled by some shares of companies, for example, Apple or Amazon or Google, and then you own a small piece of that company. And when the value of that company goes higher, you can cash out, you can earn commissions or every single year they pay some dividends. So you will earn some passive income.

Also, many companies in the US pay dividends every four months. So let's say that every four months you get 100 dollars, 100 dollars. What are her dollars? All you need to do is just to invest in some of these companies, put your money there and hold the shares. And then a lot of websites are going to do this. You can just Google the best stock brokers in your country. If you are living in the U.S., you can type best stock brokers in the U.S. If you are living in, for example, Germany, you can type in your own language to find the best stock brokers, then read the reviews, and find the best ones.

And before you start putting some money in, I recommend that you grab some, for example, two or three bestsellers about stock market investing. So you understand the basics, how you can make money with this stock market investing is pretty simple. My personal recommendation is that you diversify your portfolio, meaning that you buy several big ones for a smaller amount of money and then you just hold them for life.

So you just buy them and you keep them forever. You don't do trading, you don't buy and sell, you don't buy and sell. You just buy. You hold them forever. And this is not official investment advice. This was my personal recommendation. So don't take it like you must do it immediately. It is just my personal opinion and recommendation. It has brought the work over the time Book. And that's also what let's say most successful investors seem to recommend.

Also, Warren Buffett, one of the richest men in the world. He says for an average investor, the best way is to buy so-called diversified mutual funds. So you buy a piece of a mutual fund, meaning that you get the small share of all the big ones. So you get some Apple, you get some Google, you get some Amazon, you get a small piece of everything by investing in this kind of mutual fund. So this was just a very short description of what the stock market is investing in. How are you going to get started? I recommend that you research more, but this really is all about giving ideas. How you can make passive income and stock market investing is definitely the easiest way. The only thing you need to do is click a couple of times and then you can start earning some passive income.

The drawback is that you probably need some capital to get started. And the second thing is that if you want to earn a lot of money, you also need a lot of money. And the income is not so high compared to these other resources that I'm going to explain in a moment. So stock market investing in the long term, it's not very risky in the long term. It seems that things go up and up and up all the time . If you take a look at the last 150 years, you'll see that things are going up and up all the time. The second one is more riskier. That's called crypto currencies. I have invested in cryptocurrency already since 2015. As you have seen, they have gone up and up and up, but sometimes they have been crashing. So cryptocurrency is much more riskier, the stock market investing, but they can also make much higher returns.

For example, my record back in the days I made like 50000 euros in two months, however, I didn't sell it. I sold some of it. Then I bought some risky cryptocurrency and. I lost almost that whole 50000 euros quite fast, so that's what can happen. So that's an example that really illustrates to you how much you can make and also lose with cryptocurrency. So be careful if you would ask for my opinion. Where should you invest in cryptocurrency?

Because there are so many different ones. My recommendation would be to buy Bitcoin, hold it for a long term and then never sell it. Basically said it when the value is like one million per bitcoin or something like that, if you want to earn passive income with cryptocurrency. There are also some of them, for example, Banchero that I'm holding myself that pays you some dividends or for example, Bynum's Koide. So they have a cryptocurrency for their crypto exchange. And every time somebody uses their exchange, every time somebody uses their platform, their website, you earn some small commissions for that. And there are also some other types of cryptocurrency that can earn passive income. Some of them are very simple, some of them are complicated.

My recommendation is that if you don't understand how it works, don't invest. If you understand and you feel it's good that you understand the basics and you do the research, then you can invest, but make sure that you understand. But the group is something very volatile. You can make a lot of money or lose a lot of money. But this is one of our seven passive income ideas. The third one I want to mention, which is much more stable, is if you want to earn a stable income that grows and grows and grows, grows, basically every single month, you start earning more from affiliate marketing. And I am also doing it myself. That's my main source of income currently.

It means that you will make money by promoting someone else's product. And how you can do this automatically is, for example, writing blog posts or creating videos. And when somebody clicks your link and buys something, you will earn a commission. So, for example, I have a YouTube channel. I have lots of videos there. Every time somebody clicks the links and goes and buys something, I earn a commission or I have a blog post where I have more than 700 blog posts on my blog. And every time somebody goes there, click something and buy something. I earn a commission for that so you can earn money while you are sleeping or doing whatever you want.

I learned affiliate marketing through the community called Wealthy Affiliate, and afterwards I have honed my skills even more through the training called Legendary Marketer. And I got started as a complete beginner and I learned to make a living online with affiliate marketing and I have seen that anybody can do it. So that's definitely something very interesting and inspiring. The benefit with affiliate marketing is also that you have full control of the stock market. You cannot really control what happens, though. Things may go up or they go down or cryptocurrency. They may do basically everything in the world with affiliate marketing.

You control, you can control to promote, you can control where you promote it, how much you promote. What do you do? You have full control over your income. If you want to earn more, you can do more. So with affiliate marketing, I like that you can really control your income. So that's one of the biggest benefits. And also the income potential is huge once you start doing and learning. So I leave you a link to the description of where you can learn more about it. The next one that I want to mention is called real estate investing. And that's also what I mentioned during the intro, mentioning that every single month I get 500 dollars to my bank account just by checking out my phone because I have bought an apartment in Finland, my whole country, and every single month the tenant pays me the rent and I own money for that like this. And the more apartments you buy, the more money you will earn like this.

Of course, you will need to pay for maintenance of the apartment. But I will say that real estate investing is one of the most popular ways in the world to earn passive income. It's like passive income, one or one, or let's say old school, because it's so popular. It has been there for years or even hundreds of years. You buy our apartment and then rent it to somebody else or let's say you buy an office space and you rent it to a company and you earn money for that. And the benefit with this one is that once you have done like both apartments and then you have rented it to somebody, then it's easy. Like it takes some effort to research apartments in an area and do all this kind of stuff.

This takes effort. But once you have bought it, once you have somebody living there and paying the rent, then it starts to become easier. One drawback with real estate investing is, Of course, that it requires more capital because you cannot just buy a house without money, something you need some money. And usually you will need to go to the bank and ask for a loan, also for financing and for the. I think you may need some say so that you can be part of the apartment. So let's say for people who are broke, this is not the best way. But once you start earning some money, then this can be a great way to earn some more passive income, little by little. And Of course, with real estate investing, because now we are usually talking about some bigger money.

I recommend that you research very well before you get started to do your research. And then you study and you learn. You ask from some of the more experienced people and then you start doing because otherwise you might just lose money in bad deals, on the other hand. I would also say it's just get in the game because that's how you learn any of these seven ways to make passive income losers get in the game you start doing and then you start learning by doing what with the real estate, the mistakes that you make, they will be more expensive. So that's why I recommend that you research very well before you get started researching the area where they want to buy it and compare the prices, calculate the apartment, calculate the cost, calculate income.

Because, Professor, are real estate investors, they say that purchases are made with the calculator. They are not made with the heart or mind or something abstract like this. You make purchases with your calculator, you calculate that everything works well, and then you buy it and then you rent it further and then you start earning this passive income. That's how it works in a nutshell. Very much for reading. And see you in the next video. How wonderful. Wonderful day.

3 More Ways To Earn Passive Income!

And then something that you don't need so much capital is following a YouTube channel, because if you have a smartphone or if you have a webcam, you can start a YouTube channel right away. You don't actually even need a webcam if you just have a microphone. You can start filming your screen or recording your voice, adding images and clips, and then you can start a YouTube channel. So this is one of the, let's say, low barrier ways to start earning passive income through YouTube.

You can make money through the ad revenue. So when somebody reads your video and they click the ads that show up before the video, you will earn commissions or if you leave some promotions in the video, some affiliate links that I mentioned earlier, you will always earn some commissions and earn some money. So starting a YouTube channel is a wonderful way to earn some passive income nowadays. And I would say that it will grow and grow because it's becoming more and more popular all the time.

And the last two ways that I mentioned may be a little bit surprising for you to make pastie income first to fund this by hiring other people. So you pay somebody to do something for you so you will earn money while he's working, like based on his work or her work, you will earn money. And the more people you have working for you, the more passive income you can earn. Think about Jeff Bezos or Mark Zuckerberg or Bill Gates. They have hundreds of thousands. There are tens of thousands of people working for them and they earn passive income through that.

And Of course, you can do it on a smaller scale. What a person is working for you two persons, three persons for business, and that's all passive income to your pocket. Of course, you need to calculate, like, how much does it cost to hire somebody and how much revenue or income will that make for you and do all these calculations again with the calculator. But this is something that some people may not think about right away. When they think about making passive income. You can either put the money work for you in the stock market or you can put it work into other people. And a nice thing with this one is, Of course, that you may also provide some work for somebody. So you make a service for them so it can be something great for them as well. And nowadays I want to mention something inspiring and exciting because the world has opened like nowadays.

It's so much easier to find people because you have the Internet and you can hire people from the countries where the cost of living is lower for a much cheaper price than you could pay in, let's say, more expensive countries. For example, often when you go to websites where you find people, people who are in the United States, you can be guaranteed that they will ask a much higher price, even though their skills would not be better. So that's what I have noticed. Like somebody in the United States, they would not have any skills. But still they ask for, let's say, twenty dollars per hour. Then you see somebody, for example, from the Philippines. They have a great skill sometimes and they are asking only for ten dollars per hour.

Can you see the difference? Like somebody in the Philippines, they have much better skills and he's asking less money than the person in the United States. That's just because they have been used to different kinds of salaries and the cost of living is different. So I highly recommend that you do the research a little bit and open a little bit, not only hire the people from your country, but also from other places where the cost of living might be lower. So you do a service for them by hiring them and then you also grow your own business. So it's a win-win situation for both. And last but not least, this is interesting.

Borrowing money, borrowing money can make you passive income. Let's say that somebody needs, for example, ten thousand dollars and you have ten thousand dollars. You borrow the money from him and then you sign a contract or a paper that you agree with him that he will pay you something every month to pay the money back. And then you agree to some interest that he will pay, for example, five percent interest on that loan. And little by little, you will earn some interest in that. And this is also why you are helping the other person because he needs that, for example, building his business or something in his life.

And at the same time, if you are earning some money or if you need money for yourself, you can offer somebody else an opportunity to earn passive income by borrowing money from you. Then you've got to invest into your business and earn more money with that money that you have borrowed from somebody else. Very much for reading. And see you in the next video. How wonderful. Wonderful day.

Step-By-Step Tutorial

My friend, take a look at this, honey. Twenty dollars, honey, can send twenty three dollars here, honey, and twenty dollars, 50 cents. You have been asking me to show you easy ways to make money online. And in my personal opinion, honey, guess it's one of the easiest ways to make money from home. In this video, I will show you three steps that you need to do to start making money. And I will give you a five dollar bonus if we read this video. And so follow my instructions very carefully to start making money with honey games. But the first step to start making money with Hannegan is to go to their website or download their app or with your Android device.

And I give you this five dollar bonus when you use my code Ropen five or use it to link it with scripts and to sign up. So simply click the link with scripts and you go to Hanigan website. Then the second step is you will sign up and log in to this website. I will show you in a moment how much money you can actually earn with this. But first, let's go through this step so it will click here, sign up and login and it will take you to this page. And here you will sign up this blue button right here. And then you need to fill out your email address and create your password, as you have done. That now comes to a very important part.

You will click here, redeem coupon code, and here you will click and copy and paste my code roll by five. This will give you a five dollar sign up for both. Next step is to sign up and now you are already inside the Hanigan members area. You will see here that you have this five dollar sign up bonus here. And the next step that you need to do is to confirm your email. So you simply click here, confirm email, and need to call your inbox, for example, Gmail. They send you this email. Welcome aboard. It's great to have you here.

First things first, verify your email. We will simply click this blue button here or this link here, and then your email is verified and you can get started. Now that you have verified your email, you come back here to Hanigan and then you will download again and get started. So if you are using Windows, you will download the Windows app. If you are using a Mac, you will download it. And if you are using an Android phone, then you will download an Android application. I am personally using Macs, so I will simply click here, download the Mac OS app and then it will start downloading and I will show you what happened.

So Open App Store, then I simply install the app, I use my I.D. and then it will move forward. It will start installing and downloading this application and this is what happens. Person Safe Application. It has been around already for a while and you can read already to conceal the Internet. This is a legitimate and a safe way to earn money online. You can find many reviews. I will. Saw you also in a moment that many people are using this, like thousands of people from all over the world worldwide are using this app to make money online. So now I'm downloading it. And here it explains how you can make extra money with this. So it works like this. Sariel Internet can earn your Mac money when it's connected through your Wi-Fi or Internet.

So when you are connected to the Internet, this will earn you passive income with this data that you will share with and then click next and here earn more on all devices. It's all Hanigan on your favorite devices. Make sure they are connected to different networks and APIs. If you are using the same IP, then two devices is optimal. Use two devices. It will make you the maximum amount of money. Click next, invite everyone to join. Help others join Hanigan and you will get ten percent of what they earn. The more they share, the more you get. So for example, if you share your link to your friend, he earns, for example, one hundred dollars from Hanigan, you earn 10 percent. It means you earn ten dollars for sharing your link. So that's how it works.

Typical affiliate program. Then you click here next and it says, Sit back and earn. You don't have to do anything after you install Hanigan. Just keep the app on and let your earnings grow. So I will show you the launch on Startup and click here start. Hannegan is good to go. It will run now quietly on the right side of the menu bar. That's how easy it is. Let me show you what it looks like so you can also earn some bonuses. So if you want additional credit you can enable this option right here. Let me show you here now it's active. So it has been started and you can see the balance here, obviously, as I started it.

Now it shows zero zero zero credits. But if you take a look at further and later, it will start gathering you those credits. And once you have enough credits, you can go back to Hanigan applications inside the members area. And when you reach the payout limit missile here, which is twenty dollars, then you can turn those credits into cash and you can cuss out through PayPal. That's also true in the beginning. Twenty dollars. Fifty cents earned. Twenty three dollars earned. And you can also see another payment for twenty dollars earned here. You will find dozens and dozens of payment pools on the Internet from other people who have used this Hanigan application. So. A real app, and they have this minimal payout, which is 20 dollars now, you might be asking how much money you can earn with this, as you saw in these payments proves they are not like huge money.

It's not like thousands of dollars. You can say twenty dollars here and to twenty dollars and fifty cents, something like that. Not huge money. So Hannegan is not going to make you rich. That kind of. I can make sure it's not some of those big ways to make money online. Like I have Sony you on my YouTube channel. It's more like pocket money, some side income because I said this is one of the easiest ways to make money online. You simply share your Internet connection and your data and you will start earning passive income. And as you have learned on my YouTube channel in my other videos, Easy Ways to make money don't usually pay so much. If you want to earn like thousands of dollars, then you usually need to learn some skills and provide something different. But if you want to earn easy money by sharing your Internet connection like passive income, then it will be a little bit less. If you want to increase your earnings with Hannegan, you can, Of course, always go here to invite friends and you can copy and paste the link.

You can share it to your friends and followers on social media. And when they sign up and when they start earning on

Hanigan, you can earn 10 percent of that. So Of course, that's one way to increase your earning, as with other websites, as you have seen on my YouTube channel. Now, you also might be asking how they are using your Internet connection? Because you will make money by sharing your Internet connection. So let me show you here. Here they basically explain how Hannegan works. They use this, for example, price comparison, brand products on SEO and Web intelligence, Web Fraud Protection AD.

What if it goes in so many different things because it's 100 percent safe to use? They have secured the system. Let me also read for you here, honey, against up connection is inaccessible by outsiders and its fully encrypted guarantee during private information is unreachable so nobody will get your private information. We don't collect any personal data about our users because we simply don't need that. The one and only thing you share with your hand against the network is the Internet connection. And, this was mentioned before. You earn money for it. So your earnings will depend on how much data you share with them so you can be rest assured and make money from home without any security threats.

Again, one thing to consider is how much you are paying for data. If you are paying a lot of money for data, then it may not be worth it for you. But if data is free for you, for example, monthly packets, then Of course this will be one way to earn money simply through Internet connection and you start earning money again. The five dollar bonus that you can immediately start using with Hannegan can pass this. We take this code and start using it to get that five dollar bonus. But let me show you again a couple of other areas so you can see that other people are also using you can see on a trust pilot, most people are giving it excellent rating. Of course, there are some people who gave it one star, but it's usually those people who think that they are going to become rich quickly. This app. No, this is not something like this. This will make you some little money, some pocket money, but it's not going to make you rich.

People who understand that this is just for small side income, then those give you a five star review. You can see also here, it has generated three hundred and ninety seven upvotes for search on Google. Like Hannegan reviews. You can see that the average today is like four point three stars out of five out of twenty two votes. So most of the people love this app. Of course, some people, if they want to or like thousands of dollars or something like that, they are not going to enjoy this so much because this is more like a site income, some small money. But there again, you have been asking for easier ways to make money online. So here you go.

This is one of the easiest ways to make money. Simply follow the link groups and then download this application to your computer or your Android phone and then start using this, then enable them through your Internet connection. Then you can start earning some little money passively. In other words, you can make money while you are sleeping. If you have any questions about Hanigan, make sure to leave a comment. I will be more than happy to reply to you and help you out personally. As you have seen. I reply to all of your comments personally. I read them through. So thank you very much for reading this video. And you and me and my friend, we will see you in the next video. How wonderful. And a successful day, my friend.

How Much Does This Pay?

In this Hannagan review, I'm going to come out again, money from Hanigan, as you can see. Twenty dollars. I'm going to give you this five dollar bonus and I'm going to explain to you how much you can really earn from Hanigan, by the way, when you take this five dollar bonus? I don't have any money for this. It's only for you.

You earn five dollars immediately for that, not me. Because in my previous Hanigan case, out of a video that I showed you on Matsuno, I saw you click by Click How to put money from this website. And somebody said, OK, I'm going to give you five dollars by using your link. No, no, I don't earn five dollars. When you use Marlink, you earn five dollars.

I start earning money on Hannegan only once you start earning. So that's how it works. So let me tell you, you simply click here, request pay out and then are you ready to collect twenty dollars? You click your request, pay out and then it downloads for a while and after a while it says it's processed and later on you will be able to receive the money to your PayPal account. So I'm going to show you how much money different people have been earning with this website and how you want money you can earn with Tanigawa.

The first thing, if you want to get started, you simply claim this five dollar bonus. And as I told you in my previous winners, once you start earning money from Hanigan, that's only when I as I explained in my previous Hanigan with my YouTube subscribers, who are basically tomasello to make honest money online, have earned hundreds and hundreds and hundreds of dollars in total from happening again. I know that because they signed up through my link and once they started earning, that's also when I earned money. So it's like a win-win situation. When you win, I win also. So let me show you now different estimates here on Quora. Somebody asked how much money you will earn and they say that they said if you run Hanigan 24 hours, which is seven hundred and twenty hours a month, you can make fifty dollars per month. So that is one estimate. But now there are different factors that affect your earnings.

One is, for example, Internet speed, your latency and data throughput. I believe you Lincolnesque groups are for these articles if you want to read more details from Hanigan blog. But obviously, if you have a faster Internet connection, faster Internet speed, then you can earn more money. Because let me show you here, somebody commented on this under this video that he only let me tell you, I am using Wi-Fi and I am running Hanigan for all time, 24 hours a day, but maximum, only 20 cents per day. I am getting Kamahl Raj. I'm not sure, but I guess this is India, something from Asia based on the name. But I would guess that the internet connection is not very fast if he earns 20 cents per day. For example, let me hear this person and take Hasner. They also say that you could earn maybe around one dollar per day.

DeCastro actually I think has some proof of that. So that would be like thirty dollars per month and not like it would be five times more than twenty cents per day. But that is because of the Internet speed that it would affect. Also, if you are using limited data, then it's not recommended to use, in my personal opinion, only having unlimited data plans because then you can earn passive income. You simply download the app, let it run in the background, and it will make your money automatically. So that's my recommendation.

Fifty dollars per month. I would say that this is probably maximum if you are using only this Internet connection. But Of course they also have other ways to earn psychodramas. So your referral system, if you refer your friends and they start earning and that's also one way and also content, the delivery fees are. So there are a couple of factors. I believe you linked with groups and for this article that's been explained to you, Of course, you want to set it up properly. It takes around, let's say, three or five minutes. So if you have a, let's say, slow Internet connection, it would be around twenty cents per day or let's say zero point twenty per day. And if you want to earn that twenty dollars first, you will get that five dollars for free by using my link below.

Then you need to earn fifteen dollars. And if we divide that fifteen by twenty, it would take seventy five days. To us out to gas out that 20 dollars or 75 days with the slow Internet connection, if you have a faster Internet connection, let's say you have a fast Internet connection and you are earning that 50 dollars per month, let's say 50 dollars per month. That would be around if we calculated the calculator. That would be around twelve point seven dollars per day. And if you want to earn that first twenty dollars, let's say you earn five dollars by using my bonus, you need to earn fifteen dollars more.

We divide that one by 15, divided by one point seven. It would take around eight to nine days to gas out your first twenty dollars. So you can see the difference is big. Like if you are very fast, you can earn maybe even an eight in one week. This one, if you use a slow one, it can be two and a half months. So it depends on an Internet connection. Of course, if you use this referral system, like when people sign up, they can earn even faster than even more and then you would need to use their own. So that's another thing to keep in mind. Let's say that we use this. Intermediate interconnection, so there is a third scenario that we saw there.

Let's say you are earning one dollar per day that Hossler and these guys were earning. Then you get five dollars immediately by using my bonus unit to earn fifteen dollars to cash out more. And if one dollar per day, that would be 15 days to Casal. So around two weeks. So there are people, in my personal experience, who are following MAZZARELLA and who are using Hanigan. They are usually countries from Nigeria, Philippines, India, Ghana, these kinds of countries. So I would say on average, the interconnection is a little bit slower than, for example, in Finland, which is my home country.

I would say that it's a little bit slower than what we saw here. It's probably slower. And Of course, you may have a fast interconnection. But let me show you now the average Sungai says that the average time to twenty dollars is forty eight days. I would estimate that I'm not sure if this counts as a five dollar bonus or not, but if it doesn't count, then it's probably even faster because you get these five dollars immediately. Let me also point out that they have paid more than half a million dollars, 500,000 U.S. dollars. So it's very reliable.

4 Apps That Give Money Automatically Once You've Activated

Now you will see seven apps and websites that will make you money while you are sleeping. Most of these apps will start making you money immediately on autopilot after you simply activate them on your mobile phone or on your computer. My favorite app for making money online is No.7 because it can make you even afford some and pay for all your living costs, rent, food, travel and all these other things. Let's start with the first one that you probably already know, because this application has paid thousands of dollars in total to my YouTube subscribers.

And I have also cussed out around 500 dollars from this automated income app, and that is called honey game. When you use Honegger, you can cash out money through your PayPal account or to Bitcoin. So it works worldwide in Europe, Africa, Asia, America, everywhere in the world. You simply need to download the application activated and it will start making you a little bit of money on autopilot. I will explain to you more in detail in my hand again playlist, which I also saw you call Hanigan tricks, how you can make even more money with Honey Game. So make sure to check out my full Hanigan playlist if you want to learn step by step, click by click how to use this and how to increase your earnings. And I saw you also a lot of payment proof when I'm cashing out money from

Hannigan and how my YouTube subscribers are earning money using this application.

Number two is also well known for my YouTube subscribers, and I know that many of you have already used this application for making money, and that is called Group the tab. You can use this on your smartphone as well as on your computer, and it will give you a free Bitcoin daily. Once you cuss out the Bitcoin, you can either keep it in the Bitcoin or you can also transfer it into your local currency using some of the cryptocurrency marketplaces so you can get it eventually in Euro USD or Filipinas or whatever is your local currency. This application works worldwide and this is one person free to use as all the other apps in this list as well. This works worldwide and you can use this for five percent free. But let's more immediately, number three, and that is called packet stream. That is very similar to Hanigan. They sell the unused Internet data in the marketplace and they pay you money for doing that.

However, packet stream is a little bit different than the Tav or Hanigan because you can only use it on your computer at the moment based on Merisotis packets. Stream is the oldest one in this industry. It's not the oldest one of these companies in our list today, but it's the oldest one of these Sariel unused Internet connections and makes money with that. So it's a very established and reliable company. Number four in our list is called Hanie Minor. With this application, you will also be undermining free Bitcoin. And once you have cashed out that free Bitcoin, you can again transfer it into your local currency. Or, Of course, you can hold that Bitcoin if you believe that the value of Bitcoin will keep on going up the Hanım line. There is a little bit similar cryptocurrency mining up like crypto tap.

It's really easy to use and you will be sharing your unused computer power with them. Honey miner will automatically optimize the mining for you so you don't need to have technical knowledge, unlike if you do regular mining with your own mining rig and all this kind of stuff. I want to mention transparently that personally I have not yet used honey miner, but I have seen many YouTube brass using it and they have been cussing out money from Honey Miner. But there are also some negative reviews of Honey Miner on the Internet. So before you start using it, do your own research and then decide if this is the best one for you.

That being said, I think most of those negative comments come from people who think that they will become rich immediately with this. They think that they simply click a button and a lot of money will start coming in. But they don't realize that automatic income apps will not make you rich quickly. Only if you use the No.7 can you make yourself rich, but not quickly. Usually before we move the number of foreign tourists and the honey miner and honey again, they are not related to each other, even though both of these have this. Honey, I just want to mention that if you are wondering, number five is.

3 More Automatic Income Apps

Number five is fluid stack, and it's a little bit similar to honey gain, but instead of earning Bitcoin, you will be earning U.S. dollars when you rent your computing power for these applications. Many of my other neighbors have asked me to review fluid stacks already. But the reason why I haven't read the video about this is that they require a little bit more than Hanigan or Honey Minor, for example.

Those apps you can start using immediately with your computer or Hannegan, you can start making money with your smartphone, but fluid's that requires a little bit more nowadays. In the past, individual users were able to use this with one computer, for example. But nowadays they require a minimum of 10 computers in order to start using them. So they have a little bit higher requirement. Then you can go to their website and fill out the application and then you can start making money. But you need more than just one device. And that's why I didn't create the video before, because I know that many people like myself don't have 10 devices laying around like that. And by the way, you can make money with many devices.

Also with Honea gain or Krypto tap, you can connect all your devices to increase your earnings anyway. So let's move to number six, and that is Speed Network and PAE Network. The reason I mention this is because so many of you have asked me about these apps and I know that there's also a lot of demand in the marketplace regarding these applications. People are wondering, can you make money with this? I also created videos about both of them. But my opinion is that these apps are not as reliable as the other ones in our list, because when you download these apps, you will be earning free cryptocurrency, you will be earning betokens and pay tokens. However, at the moment, you cannot trade those tokens in the marketplace. The value is zero and with the tab or Hannegan, you will be earning currency that has already value in the marketplace.

For example, Bitcoin or a U.S. dollar. So you can already buy things with those currencies. But we'd be talking to a spy network. You cannot get by, but in the future they may have some value, so you may download them and see how it goes. I personally don't have high hopes regarding them, but I have recently downloaded Be Network and I will be following how it goes. Now, I would say the best app for making money while you are asleep, and that is YouTube. Your income with a YouTube app can be much, much, much higher than any of these applications that I mentioned in this list on YouTube.

You can earn money through many different income sources, for example, affiliate marketing. So when people click your links and they buy something online or they take certain action online. Second, you can earn money from ad revenue when people click ads on your videos. Third, you can earn money for sponsored videos for what you can earn money from merchandise channel membership Patria. And there are many different ways you can make money with the YouTube app.

Personally, I have learnt lots of YouTube money making tricks on letting market their community, so I highly recommend to get started also with letting market share. Their program made me up to 3000 dollars in a day. That is my record with little markets there and to have a seat on my team and many other people have also made lots of money, thanks to Leslie Market there. So it's really wonderful. They have this 15 day online business builder where every single day you will be making progress and moving forward. You will also get real life support from a real person. You will be able to ask questions through a mobile phone, through WhatsApp and let the market staff members.

1st Way to Make Money While You Are SLEEPING!

Now, you will learn four ways how I earn passive income online even while sleeping and how you can make money, too. And now we are talking about lighting up not only some small pocket money. You can use these steps to make even 100 dollars per day, even 200, even 300 dollars per day, passive income while sleeping. And to be completely transparent with you. I use these tips to make more money while I'm sleeping than I used to in my nine to five jobs in the past while I was working full time. So these are super powerful.

And the last thing that I'm going to show you in this video, it's probably the most powerful one. So what is really very carefully until the end? But let's get started right away with the first way to earn passive income online, and that is blogging. Recently, I created a video where I saw eight examples of websites that are making automated money for their creators. And that gives you a good idea how this process works. But let's recap this process. First of all, you will choose a topic that they want to write about in your blog.

Personally, I recommend that it's something that you are passionate about. For example, if you like self development, you can write about personal development and all these kinds of things. If you like photography, then you can write about photography, all kinds of cameras, the right equipment and so on and so forth. If you like playing guitar, then you write about that so you choose a topic that you are passionate about.

Second thing is to simply write the blog post, write articles. For example, if your blog is about guitar, you, for example, create a guide. This is how you can get started playing guitar.

This is the best guitar, in my opinion. And then one of the most exciting parts is that when you have written those blog posts, you can leave their links and apps. So when somebody comes to a website to learn about things, they can, for example, click those ads or they can click links. For example, let's say that you have written a blog post about the best guitars and you recommend that they are the best in your opinion. When somebody clicks your links and they go and buy that guitar, you earn money from that. And the links can take people, for example, to Amazon or to some other trusted website.

So you don't need to sell anything because they leave a link or not and you will start earning money for each click if you want to learn to make money step by step with blogging, I create the comprehensive like a chapter in that we also you click by click how you will be creating your own book and know when we are talking about making passive income, we are soon going to move to number two, three and four ways how you can make money. But I want to explain a mistake that I made personally when I got started. And also I know that many people have made the same mistake. They have these expectations that you will just click some buttons and you will earn money.

For example, you create a blog and it immediately starts making your money. No, earning passive income doesn't work like that. Think about the people who are the most passive income in this world. For example, Bill Gates, Jeff Bezos, Mark

Zuckerberg, they are making billions of dollars, massive incomes. If they would stop working, they would still keep on making billions of dollars. But those are some of the most hardworking people in the world. For example, Bill Gates said that he never took a day off in his twenties, like from twenty years old to thirty years old for ten years, every single day he was working.

And usually I would guess that probably more than twelve hours and now I'm making billions of dollars of passive income. And that's usually how passive income works. Like you need to do some work beforehand and it doesn't work. Like you will make money by clicking buttons. You need to do some work. And people who work the hardest, they usually earn more money. I want to make this very clear because I had unrealistic expectations, but passive income is wonderful. As I told you, I make more passive income. So more money. Well, I was thinking about what I made in my previous nine to five job, so it's wonderful. And I recommend it for you as well.

2nd & 3rd Ways How I Made a Life-Changing PASSIVE Income Online!

The number two that I use is tick tock, and actually I also use Tick for fun and so on and so forth, I could actually make more money if I would optimize it. But here are the basic steps that you can make money out of. Step number one is to choose a topic. And again, similar phrases like with bloating to something that you're passionate about to something that you like, and then start creating videos on the topic. And then you publish those short videos.

People will see your videos and you can leave some affiliate links in your profile. And when people click your links in your Tick-Tock profile, you will earn money for that. I actually created the playlist where I explained this, making money on Tick-Tock step by step and I would leave you a link for that playlist in the description where you can learn more. But again, I mentioned that you can use them also for fun or you can use it for making money. But I must say that I have made money and I will just take a look to make money. But I also use it because it's super fun. And I'm telling this to you, like when you make money doesn't need to be something like who doesn't need to be like soha like it's going to be fun and making money and making money on Broadway.

You can do something you love and something fun. So that's what I also want to tell you. Doesn't need to be so hard. Stresa number three is YouTube and this is one of the most powerful ways, in my opinion, because when you publish videos on

Tick-Tock and they stay there, there are other reasons that they can stay a couple of months. So if you publish a video today, it can make you passive income for some months, for example. But if you publish a video on YouTube, it can make you money for years to come. I have so many new examples on this YouTube channel where I actually saw you, how I made it and how other people have made it.

So the first step to making money on YouTube is to choose a topic again. What you want to talk about, you don't want to talk about a million different topics. You want to go to something specific and something that you are passionate about, something that you like creating videos about. And the second you simply publish videos within that topic, Of course, we could go more into detail. And in some of my videos I explain in more details, I extend you the steps. I recommend reading these seven tips for making money on YouTube. There are many different ways you can earn money.

For example, YouTube pays you money for ads. So when people see your videos and they see the ads before your videos and they click them, you will earn money for that. And also on YouTube, one of the most powerful ways is with affiliate marketing. So you leave a link and description of your video and people click it. They go somewhere and buy something. You earn money. For example, if you create a video with your smartphone, you can leave a link and a description and say, this is the smartphone that I use to create this video. Then you have a link to Amazon. People go to Amazon and they take a look at that smartphone. They buy it from Amazon. Amazon will pay you money. The same with any other thing.

Let's say you use a camera for recording YouTube videos. Who will tell people this is the camera that I used. I love it because this and this and this. They go to Amazon or other websites. They buy something. You earn money. And usually people who have YouTube channels, based on my experience, they earn more money from affiliate marketing than from YouTube ads. So that's very powerful. And also YouTube, you can promote, for example, your own Books, your own products. So if you already have some products that you want to promote, you can promote them through your YouTube channel.

And I think this is one of the ways to make even the highest income from YouTube. And I promise to tell you in the end, number four, which is super powerful, like number three, number two. Number three, they are powerful strategies to make money. But no, for many entrepreneurs and many business owners say that this is probably the most powerful strategy for making money for similar reasons.

Most Powerful Way to Earn Passive Income!

Email marketing, so collecting on is sending them automated messages and making money by doing that. When I heard about email marketing for the first time, I remember there was this intermarket that I called Chris Farrell and he told me that he said that email to his list. Then he went to the movie theater and he was in a two hour movie during that two hour movie. He made like thousands of dollars for that one email that he sent to that list. And I know that it's true because many other people are also doing the same. So how does e-mail marketing work?

Let's say that you have, for example, the Ticktock or Utapao Block or some other channel. You can direct people to your email list. So you provide the people something in return for their email. For example, if your topic is, for example, playing guitar, you can tell them there are seven people who play guitar. But your e-mail address here and then you will send that guide. And when you have their email address, you can then send them emails, for example, where you provide more tips for playing guitar. And then you can also promote, for example, some guitar playing Books or some guitar products.

And that's how you can make money and you can make money with email marketing within any industry. And there are at least two reasons why email marketing is super powerful. You will have 100 percent control because if you make money on YouTube or take stock, they may change the rules. They may say, OK, we will ban, we will say something, and then you cannot use them anymore with Ima's. If you have somebody's email address, you have one percent control.

Nobody can take that away from you. So many of us will say that if you have your email list, that is your business like that has huge value to email. It can have a value of tens of thousands, even hundreds of thousands of dollars if you keep on building it for a longer period of time. Second thing is that studies say that email marketing gives huge returns for business owners because there are many businesses that invest money in, let's say, social media, marketing, video marketing, all kinds of marketing.

But over and over again, I have seen many studies that say email marketing gives the highest returns. And I can also confirm that from my own experience doing email marketing, it gives huge returns. And you will be my friend. We will see you in the next video. What A wonderful day, my friend.

The FP Model

I want to create the video where I saw you more passive in some ways from a five million dollar entrepreneur, Pat Flynn. By the way, in 2008, he already created a five million dollar entrepreneur. So assume that now he's already an almost 10 million dollar entrepreneur. But Faloon makes most of his money while he's sleeping. So we call this passive income and he says that there are three proven passive income models that anybody can start using today.

And those are called the FP model, the AA model and the EPI model. And in this video, I'm going to explain to all of those three passive income workers, one by one. So you can start making money online starting today. Another reason why I wanted to create this video is because many of you asked me, can you show me some legit YouTube tuberose? Because there are lots of these fake YouTubers who make money unless paid like Big Makarand Red Richard Branson, who are liars. But Backplane is one of the legitimate ones. So you can follow him. And in this way I would give it to you three of his basic income.

Starting right the way with no one. And that is the FP model if P stands for freelance and product model. And let me explain to you how it works. He says that this is the best way for those of you who want to earn money faster, you want to make some quick money. And actually, many of you have been asking me to find out what is the fastest way to make money. And I would say starting as a freelancer is a good way because once you get hired by a company, you can start earning money. In a nutshell, it means that you need to have some skill that you provide for a company and they will pay money for that. For example, a graphic design or writing or photography or video editing or whatever is your skill you provided for a company and they pay you for that.

There are lots of freelance platforms. You can do this for a freelancer and go through many different websites. And also one of them is FYRIR, where you can also start making money without any skills, without any prior experience worldwide for one person free. And actually yesterday I published a video where I saw 15 five objects that everybody all around the world for one person's free can start today with zero experience, zero knowledge, so anybody can start making money online. So, OK, now we are talking about freelancing.

You might be asking, but we are going to make money when I'm sleeping. Yes, you are completely right. And that's why Patston explained how you can turn those freelance jobs into passive income. Let's say that you are providing a service. You are doing, for example, social media management for some companies, for example, a place where you start making passive income is, for example, hiring other people to do the work for you. So then you get the order from the company, they pay you some money, and then you have some other freelancer or an employee and they will do the work for you. So then you will earn money while you are sleeping or you can create in a park. Also, you give a certain system for companies to follow.

You say, here is my product, follow this and you will get more like clients or more views or the social media, for example. And then they start using that. That is your product. You will start earning passive income. So you can first start by learning and earning as a freelancer or also as an employee. You learn to make a skill better and you earn money at the same time. And then you can also hire other people, teach them to do the same, and then you can simply earn the money while somebody else is doing the work for you. That has to be a model.

The AA Model

A mother? Well, it's a model like what is this like an anonymous alcoholic or what it's like? Well, this is what it stands for. Audience and advertising models still do ask for audience advertising. I don't want to do advertising. I don't have an audience. Well, let me explain to you how you can make money with this. First, you will build an audience. And if you are saying to me, but I don't have an audience, I don't know what to do.

Everybody including myself also. But soon everybody starts with zero audience. So if you now have zero followers, you are starting from the same point that everybody else on this planet. And I know that in the beginning it's usually hard to build an audience, but over time it becomes easier. So let me explain to you how the money making process works. You get to pick one platform, whether it's YouTube, whether it's creating a blog or Tic-Tac channel, and then you start creating content. There is something that people want to read and they want to read or whatever is the platform. And then you will get followers there. And once you have followers, you can make money in many different ways.

Actually, some of my videos are five different ways. How are you going to make money once you have an audience, for example, with apps, with sponsors, sports, with merchandise like T-shirts or all these kinds of things, you can also make money with affiliate marketing or by creating your own product. So once you have an audience, there are so many different at least five different ways. How are you going to make money with this model? It usually works in a way like the first unit work, like you want it to work quite a long time and your income and your audience builds up little by little. But once you have an audience, you can simply create the promotion and make money immediately.

I remember this video from Chris Farrell. He built an email list and he sold his laptop computer and he said he has this email that he will send a promotional email, that email before he goes to the movies. Then he goes to the movies, shot in the window, and he stays at a movie for two hours or something like that. And after that, he takes his smartphone, his mobile phone, and he sees that he has made thousands of dollars, if I remember a thousand dollars during the two hour movie. And I was blown away. Like when I was a beginner, I was starting over looking at these characters. Whoa. Is it possible nowadays?

I know it's possible because I know a lot of people who are making that kind of money like email marketing or building audiences and all this kind of thing. So, yes, it is possible, but it takes time and everybody starts from zero. Blogging is the first platform where I start building an audience, so I simply type on my laptop and then I earn money by doing that and anybody can do it. I have done it in English, even though my native language is finished, as you can hear the accent. So you don't need to worry if your English is not perfect. You don't need to worry if you are starting from zero, everybody starts from that. So don't worry at all. You can do that if you want, but now you are already probably anxious to hear the number three percent in Gomorra IEP and I'm going to explain it in a moment.

The EP Model

Model, and that stands for expert product business model. What does it mean? Well, you place yourself as an expert in the marketplace and then you sell a product or service. Let me explain to you, for example, I know well how to play chess so I could be an expert in the topic and I could consult people. I could also create workshops or I could create books and Books. So then I would share my expertise and people will pay for that and earn money while sleeping. That's what this model is in a nutshell.

And by the way, I want to mention that you're going to turn those like active income models where you are working and earning money at the same time into passive income or else. Let me explain to you one example from Dan Henry that was also made like millions of millions of dollars online, like 30 million dollars or something like that, if I remember right. He explains that he created the workshop where he consulted people to build their businesses to the next level or something like that. And then he recorded that training, that workshop.

It was like six, six, eight hours. And then he put that workshop into a Book. So then he talked to people for a lower price and then people were able to walk by that training, simply that live recording. And Of course, afterwards, he started adding some new recordings and copying and making it like a more polished WARSAN. But they simply recorded his workshop at first and then he sold this as a Book and then people liked that Book. So that is one way or let's say that you are consulting people all the time about something. You are providing some mentoring or something like that. People are learning from you.

What if instead of doing that little one on one or let's say four or five people or 10 people, what if you would write a book about it? Or usually a Book is a better option or let's say a coaching program, because with the book, people are usually willing to pay maybe something like 10 to 15 dollars or maybe 20 dollars maximum. But if you said, Of course, some people are willing to pay even 1000 dollars, if it's like a high value Book, maybe even two thousand dollars or even the cheapest Books are usually at least the ninety seven dollars minimum or something like 200 dollars minimum. So obviously you can charge more money from Books. And actually he has made lots of money by selling his online Books. He's hosting his Books on this platform called Cuttable.

What to Do RIGHT NOW If You Don't Have Any Money to Invest?

In two days, we will. I wanted to show you and talk to you about one of the first ways that I used to make money online, and that is called investing. And specifically how I started making money online was stock market investing. In other words, I bought some shares of companies and they pay me yearly some money for owning that company, if it sounds complicated. Don't worry. I'm going to explain to you more in this video. So be sure to read this until the end. I'm going to give you at least four highly practical pieces of advice that you can use immediately to make more money with investing. So let's get started right away.

One of the most important investing advice that I can give to you is start as early as possible. The earlier you start, the better if you are now 15 years old. Start immediately. Start investing money right now if you are 20 years old, start right now if you are 30. Start right now. If you are 40. If you are 55 or 60, start right now. It doesn't matter what your age is. The best time to start investing is right now because that's how you will make the most return for your money. And now you should see in the screen two pictures that illustrate the power of compound interest. So compound interest simply means that you will earn interest on top of interest.

And this picture, especially social, where, well, how it will grow fast. If you compare simple interest and compound interest with compound interest, your income will grow slowly. But with compound interest it can skyrocket. But the important thing is that you get started as early as possible because some people, they wait and they wait and then they wait. And that's not how you do it. If you want to get advantage of compound interest and the most money with investing, you need to start immediately. The best time was to start five years ago, but the second best time is to start right now. So the first point starts immediately. Second point, if you are asking me, well, I don't have any money. How can I invest if I don't have any money?

Well, there are two ways you can either loan somebody else's money that I don't recommend. And the second way is to save some money. And this is what I recommend. Now, if you are saying, hey, drop it, but my expenses are so high, how can I invest anything? Because I don't earn, let's say, two thousand dollars every month and then I spend two thousand dollars on food and rent and everything. How on earth I could invest when there are two different ways. Now what you can do, let's say, for example, that you earn two thousand dollars per month and your expenses are two thousand dollars per month, you can either increase your earnings so you can earn 3000, 4000, 5000 dollars per month or you can decrease your expenses.

So instead of spending all the money two thousand dollars per month, you will spend, let's say, one thousand five hundred dollars per month and now you will have five hundred dollars every single month that you can use for investing, for example, in the stock market or real estate or in your own self or in your business. But that's how you do it. You either increase the earnings or decrease the expenses. And now if you are asking head, Robert, how can I do this? How can I decrease my expenses? I am already living very frugally.

Well, what I recommend usefully is to increase your earnings because, OK, you can cut your expenses a little. Maybe you do not eat outside, maybe you live in a smaller place. Then you can cut expenses a little, but you can only do it to some extent. But on the other hand, your earnings can grow and grow and grow and grow and grow without limit. There are some people who are earning 10 times more or 100 pounds more or 1000 times more. So your earning potential is unlimited. And that's why I recommend that you increase your earnings so that your earnings are higher than your expenses and you have, let's say, extra one thousand dollars every month.

What you should do is to pay yourself first. So when you get your salary, let's say three thousand dollars per month, you take some money out of it and you put it aside. You don't spend it like it's some money that you never spent. For example, you put it on a separate account and you decide this is the money that I do not touch, no matter what. And that's how little by little, it will increase your net worth, because many people think, OK, I can just take my salary that I spent here and there and there are there and there. And suddenly at the end of the month, they realize that they don't have money. But the key is to take some money out of your salary and put it aside. Immediately they call this you pay yourself first, because if you don't do this, what happens often that you end up with zero dollars?

I know some people who are very frugal, like they never spent almost any money that they cut their expenses. But those are very few people, let's say one in 20 or one in 100. So very few people can really manage their money without putting some money aside. But for most people, let's say for you or 99 percent of you, I would say that take some money immediately away and then spend the rest of your money every single month for 100 percent sure you will have at least some money aside that you can use for investing.

So that's the first step to pay yourself first. Then you will have some money for investing and now we will move into a subject: what should you do in the West where you will get the highest returns and where you will get lots of money fast, like many people asking how to get lots of money fast. Well, I will give you my best advice on that question. Now, let me tell you what happens with a lot of people I have seen first hand.

The MOST IMPORTANT Investing Video You'll Ever See!

Let's say that they take this money aside and now they have, let's say, one thousand dollars, what they will do is they look on the Internet how to make money by trading or investing in the stock. They go and sign up to some website. They put some money in the stocks. They start trading, buying and selling and buying and selling. And sometimes some of my friends come to me excited. Hey, Rob, I started this new thing. I'm trading money here. And then after some time, they come back to me and they say, hey, I lost all my money. So simply what happens here is that they start investing money or trading and they don't have any skills.

And you don't want to be this person. You first want to have some skills before you invest into anything, learn what you are investing in, learn the subject, whether it's stock market or real estate or some business, you need to learn the subject. Never invest into something that you don't understand. That's the first key and the first rule for in Western. Always study the subject first and then some people think, OK, I'm going to make a lot of money, invest in the stock market for the long term. I buy a piece of apple or a piece of Amazon and a piece of Facebook.

By the way, there are great companies. I own some of their services also. But this is the strategy for the long term that you are going to make some little bit of money. When you buy some stocks in the stock market, you can expect a good return. It's like 10 percent interest per year. So if you invest

1000 dollars, you're going to expect that it will be one thousand one hundred dollars after one year. If everything goes well, sometimes it can be more supplies, it can be less. But let's say that on average, six to 10 percent, it's on average what you will earn in the stock market. So it's really low.

And what I think about the stock market, it's like a place where you can keep some of your money and it's for low passive income, like holding some of your money. It's always better than keeping it in a bank account. But if you want to make a lot of money faster, I don't recommend the stock market. If you want to make a lot of money, I recommend that you invest in your own skills, in your own learning, and then start building your own business, because most of the really rich people in the world, they started their own businesses. If you take a look at billionaires and millionaires or super rich people, almost all of them have their own businesses.

So they make some money. Then they buy some Books. So they learn from mentors, they buy Books, and then they start putting money into their business. So what I would recommend for you is to take some area, what you want to learn, for example, Internet marketing or selling products on Amazon or, for example, drop shipping or e-commerce or any other business and start learning that skill. Take some Books. Take, for example, Books for Amazon FBA or affiliate marketing. What I personally recommend, because it's so you can start with almost no capital at all. Take some Book that will walk you through step by step how you can make money online. And when you invest your money in that Book, you will learn the skills and now you will have the skills to make some money.

For example, with affiliate marketing. And once you have the skill, then you can invest more money. For example, you can buy some tools or you can do, for example, advertisements, and then you can start putting money in your business and then you will get more money out. And in the stock market, let's say if you put in 1000 dollars, maybe you will get 1100 dollars after one year. So maybe 10 percent interest. Sometimes if you invest in your business, you'll put 1000 dollars in and you get 5000 or even ten thousand dollars out. Of course, not always. Sometimes you may lose the whole money, but the earning potential is much higher when you invest in your own skills and in your own business. And now you're saying to me like, hey, Robert. But there are people like Dave Ramsey or David Bach or some people who say that it's better to invest in the stock market than get rich slowly. That's the best way. But hey, look at this.

People like David Bach or Dave Ramsey, what they are doing is they are also building their own businesses. They are creating content. They are buying employees. They are creating books. They are buying ads. They are investing money in all kinds of things. And then they are telling people to invest in the stock market slowly. The reason why they are probably telling this is because for most people, the average person, the easiest way is to invest in the stock market and then you will hold your money there for the long term. That's easy for most people. But if you want to earn some money faster, you cannot do what most people do. You need to do something differently.

And that is also what. Those people like Dave Ramsey and these people, they are creating content, they are creating businesses and they are giving different advice for their followers. So my best investment advice is that investing your own skills invested in your own learning and your own business.

Easy Option!

If you want to take this other risk, like investing in the stock market, my recommendation for most people that invest in index funds. What does that mean is that there are so-called funds that you will put, for example, one thousand dollars, and then that fund will own a little piece of, for example, all companies in the all because companies in the U.S. or the biggest companies in the whole world. So it diversifies. So that will lower your risk. So if you buy, for example, just one company, your money is somewhat at risk. But if you buy an index fund, first of all, you don't need to spend time studying what to do.

Second, you are usually paying very low fees, like there are sometimes no fees at all or very low fees. So you don't lose money on fees. Also, it's pretty easy and it will be quite consistent. And that's what I recommend. That was also, by the way, Warren Buffett recommends for average people. Warren Buffett is the most successful investor in the world. And he says that for average people, the best way to invest money is, for example, in index funds because it's low cost, quite low risk, and it will still earn some money, little by little. But again, this is for average and also for holding your money. But if you want to get better, I highly recommend it to start building your own business. That's where it will get the biggest returns in the long term. And that's why I personally also invest most of my money in Books, in my own learning, in online marketing tools and all these kinds of things. All right.

I hope you enjoyed it so far. So let's take a little conclusion. First, you need to pay yourself first. So when you start right now, you start paying yourself first. When you get your next salary, you take some money aside. For example, 500 dollars or fifty dollars or even five dollars is better than zero dollars. What is the best investment in Western yourself? Invest in your business. What specific things should you invest in if you are starting out by, for example, some Books or books or find some Books that really know their thing, learn from then to create some business and then start buying some business tools, for example, how to build your business and start doing that, because that's how it will build wealth over the long term. And then the last but not least advice is to be in this game for the long term.

Investing is always a long term game, and those people who are in it for the short term, they will always lose people who are in it for like one month or one week. Sometimes they wind up. Most of the time they lose big in this game for 10 years, 20 years, 30 years, 50 years. That's how you will win. Have the long term perspective, not just what will happen this year or next year, the whole long term perspective. That's what I recommend to you. I mean, we will see you in the next video. How wonderful. And a successful day.

UNIQUE Opportunity!

Did you know that you and I have at the moment amazing opportunities to make money at the stock market in this window? I'm going to reveal to you how some of the best investing gurus in the world, such as Warren Buffet or John Templeton or other great ones, would make money during these times. You don't want to miss this because this opportunity may soon be gone forever. So if you want to make money right now, all you need to do is just.

Welcome back, my friend. I am Robert, and my mission is to help you to make a life to earn money. And I wanted to create this video for you because now we are living super interesting times. It is one of the best opportunities to make money in the stock market. The prices have gone down and there are such opportunities that haven't existed there for years. But before I share my thoughts and strategy with you, I want to remind you of two extremely important things. Number one, this is not an official investment advice. I only share what I do and what some of the best investors of all time are doing during these kinds of times.

You take responsibility for your own investments, Of course. So if you make tons of money following my advice, I'm not going to ask you to give me a pile of the profits. And also, if you lose some money, you are not going to come to me complaining that, hey, I followed your advice and didn't make so much money. Number two, don't trust and don't make emotional decisions because that is the way most people lose money in the stock market. They run and they make emotional decisions, evaluating all the options carefully. And the best thing that you can do right now is, Of course, to read this video until the very end. First, let me give you an overview of what is happening in the marketplace at the moment, and then I will explain to you my strategy, how I plan to make money in this current situation. When something happens in the stock market and in the economy, there is usually a ripple effect. So something happens, then other things happen, then the next things happen.

And it's like it's like a chain. It's a ripple effect. One thing affects another thing that affects another thing. And let me explain what has happened. First, this virus started in China. Then it started spreading all over the world. And little by little, stock prices started crashing. There was lots of negative news and that caused the prices to crash. Even more people started panicking and they started selling their stocks. The prices went down, down, down, down, down in the stock market. Then governments and countries started taking actions. They closed schools, they closed borders. Most of the businesses were closed and people were forced to stay at home. And for example, in the United States, there are so many unemployed people at the moment that it's even hard to understand.

A lot of people have lost their jobs. Businesses are struggling. Many businesses are going to bankruptcy, and that causes prices to drop even more. A lot of people also need to sell their stocks because they have been losing lots of depth, a lot of leverage. In other words, they have been using banks, money and other people's money to invest in the stock market. And now they need to sell it in the panic to give that money back for their loan givers. So that makes the prices go down even more. And then governments and countries, they are literally printing new money to support these businesses and to support people.

For example, the United States is giving huge amounts of money to people and businesses. And where is that money coming from? It comes from nowhere. They simply print out new money. They put a couple of zeros on their computer screen. They are creating new money. A lot of new money is coming to the economy. Banks are literally printing tons of money at the moment. Of course, these actions help companies, at least for a moment. So it helps the stock prices go up a little bit before they start going down again.

So the reality is that now the stock prices are extremely low, much lower than they were, for example, one month or a couple of months before. But now a lot of people are asking what will happen next? How can I make sure that I make money in the stock market? There's a lot of uncertainty because as I told you, people are staying at home. Businesses are closing governments and banks, they're literally printing new money. What will happen next? I'm going to spare you the fact. But there's one thing for sure.

What Will Happen NEXT?

Sooner or later, the stock prices will go up and most likely they will go up fast all the time, cause and during decades, the stock market prices have gone extremely fast after this kind of crisis. You can see that every single time when the market has crashed for a while, it has gone up very high afterwards and usually pretty fast. I readed the statistics for the last 70 years and every time it has hit the bottom, the average for this has been recent.

In the next 12 months or in the next one year, it has been rising 30 to 40 percent. So if you have invested, for example, ten thousand dollars during the next 12 months, you would make three to four thousand dollars or profit. And that is why Warren Buffett and other great investors say that you must be greedy when others are fearful. It means that when others are panicking, they say that when the blood is flowing in the streets and everybody is like, and the complete panic then is the best time to buy stocks in the marketplace because prices are down. It's like a discount in the stock market. Think about it.

When you go to a supermarket or some store during the Black Friday, you can say that, OK, prices are 30 percent cheaper or a 50 percent discount. It's the same amount as the stock market. Prices are lower. Stocks are at a discount. You can buy it for fifty dollars, something that has an actual value of 100 dollars. And people are making lots of money as a result. For more than 200 years, the stock market, everyone in the world, excluding Japan, has just once hit new records and has always recovered from the crash. And they have hit all time highs, all new records every time for 200 years. There's only one exception in Japan, ones like 20 years ago or something like that. So the chances are very high that it will happen again.

The market will recover and everything will be normal. Think about it. There was this First World War. There was a Second World War. Then there was the Spanish pandemic, Spanish flu. There have been all kinds of crises during 200 years. And always every single time the stock market has recovered and they have hit all time highs, they have hit new records. And the people who made the most money were those who bought during the crisis when the prices were low. So almost always when you buy some index, some stocks and you hold them long enough, you will make money in the long term.

So now you might be asking when is the best time to buy and its stock? Should I buy, should I buy now? Should I buy today or tomorrow or day after tomorrow or next week? Will it crash even more? Well, I have a wonderful answer for you on having specific numbers to show you some real life examples. And actually this answer is not going to. So it has been proven to work for decades and decades and decades.

EYE-OPENING Charts That Will Blow Your Mind!

The answer is that you do not need to know the right time, actually, if you try to time the market and know the best day, you may actually lose a lot of profit. Let me show you a graph now. You should see on the screen the graph that shows you if you invested ten thousand dollars in the S & P 500 index in 1980 and if you have held that money there for thirty eight years or for 1980, all the way to 2018, during those 38 years, there are approximately 9500 trading days.

Trading days means how many times and how many days the stock market has been open. So let's say that you invested 10000 dollars in the S&P 500 index in 1980. You hold it for 38 years and you don't sell it. You don't, you don't do anything. You simply keep the money there. During 38 years, your money has grown a lot, and in 2018, your money would have been more than 700000 dollars. So that's a lot of money from ten thousand dollars to more than seven hundred thousand dollars simply by keeping your money in the S&P 500 index. But now, if you missed some of the best trading days, you would have missed tons of your profits, for example, out of those 9500 trading days if you only missed five best days. So let's say that you pulled out your money and you put it back, but you missed five best trading days.

You'd have missed two hundred and fifty thousand dollars of your profit, 250000 dollars simply by losing those five best days out of 9500 days. And then if you would have missed

30 best trading days out of those nine thousand five hundred days, you would have only one hundred and fifty thousand dollars, approximately compared to more than 700000 dollars. This example illustrates the rule that if you are missing the best trading days, if you go away from the market and then re-enter, you may miss out a lot and you can try and test this with other time frames. But most of the time you will end up with the same conclusion. If you lose the best trading days, you will lose a big amount from your profits. And that's why some of the best investors in the world, Warren Buffett and all of these guys, are saying that for an average person like you and me, it's basically impossible to time the market, almost impossible to know when is the best time to buy or not.

Now, let me show you another graph. Charles Schwab studies different scenarios. And he said that if you invest in 1993, for example, and you keep your money there for 20 years, he calculated what your profits would be with five different scenarios. In the first scenario, you would have invested ten thousand dollars in the best times every year. So you have the perfect timing. In the end of those 20 years to ten thousand dollars would be eighty seven thousand dollars approximately as you can see in the picture. Then in the second scenario, you would always invest immediately when you get money at the beginning of the year, and in that case, your ten thousand dollars would have turned into more than 80000 dollars as well. Then the third scenario is that you are doing dollar cost averaging, so you are basically buying stocks every month or something like this.

In this case, you will still have around eighty thousand dollars. The fourth scenario is that you invest in the completely worth the time your timing's bad. You simply put your money there when the prices are high and you keep your money there after that. In that scenario, your 10000 dollars would have been more than 70000 dollars. Then the last option is that you stay in class investments. So you do investments where you are not putting your money in the stock market, but you are doing some alternative investments. This is the worst option. You would only have fifty thousand dollars after 20 years. So this picture should illustrate even the worst timing. Even if you are timing the market in the completely worst way, you are still making much more profit compared to a situation where you would keep all your money in class. And in my opinion, this is really mind blowing. Also you.

The oldest is that if you invest immediately, that gives you even better returns, comparing the situation where you are doing dollar cost averaging. So buying things regularly, Of course, when you are studying this graph and studying this thing from Charles Schwab, you need to keep in mind that this is a graph from a 20 year time frame. History does not always repeat itself in the stock market, but this still gives you a good idea how little actually the timing matters. You can see that the difference between the perfect timing and the worst timing is only fifteen thousand dollars. But the difference between the worst timing and the class investments is more than twenty thousand dollars. So the conclusion is that the most important thing is that you are in the marketplace, which is a much better option most of the time than keeping your investments and keeping your money in cash.

And Of course, you and I both know that it's basically impossible to time the market perfectly. It's also impossible to time the market in the worst way. So usually it's going to be something in between. We will just throw your money when you have money and then you will keep it. And now here we are, Of course, talking about long term investing. This is not about trading or this kind of thing. This is long term investing where you buy some stocks or buy some index and then you hold it for a long term.

Whats Next

So here are three things that you can learn immediately and apply immediately. Number one, after the prices have gone down significantly, they will usually go up significantly pretty fast after the crash. Number two, missing the best training days will also eat most of your profits. So you should be in the market. Number three, even the worst timing beats the car's investments. So based on all this information and based on everything, what I have studied is from the best investors in the world, I would be happy. I would be so happy to buy in this current situation when the prices have gone down and people are panicking, people are selling their stocks.

I'm happy to buy during these times. Warren Buffett says be greedy when others are fearful. In other words, buy when most people are selling. And he also has to be fearful when others are greedy. So when everyone is buying, the prices are high, then you should be fearful. Then you should not be buying in the same way. And most likely we have these special opportunities for a limited time period because after the prices jump back again, we do not have such good opportunities like at the moment. And you have probably heard about this old wisdom.

When was the best time to plant a tree? It was 20 years ago. So when is the second best time to plant a tree? It's right now. So if you haven't started investing in the stock market 20 years ago, no worries. You're going to start today. And during these times, I explicitly recommend for beginners to start buying and investing for the long term, not for trading, not for buying, selling, buying, selling, not for that. I recommend buying some index funds, for example, for the long term, for example, S&P 500, Dow Jones or index funds in other countries. So, Of course, I want to remind you that if you make tons of money by following my advice, I'm not going to ask you for part of your profit.

And in the same way, if you lose money by following my advice, you are not going to come to me like that. Hey, Rob, what happened? Why it didn't go up and this was Amul is selling my old personal opinion. I take responsibility for my own investments and you take responsibility for your investments. I always recommend that you study things. I don't always read books. What causes this? And then when you become better investors, you have better knowledge. Then you can make better investment decisions.

Why Should You Aim to Make Passive Income?

Would you like to make 100 dollars per day passive income online in this window? I'm going to show you real life examples how you can make 100 dollars per day online, even if you would be sleeping or laying down on the beds or spending time with your loved ones. In other words, how you can make money while you are not even working. Before I saw you, the steps and the struggle to see how you can make 100 dollars per day passive income online.

I want to appreciate and take time to thank you for all the comments that you have been leaving on my channel. I appreciate the lot that you ask questions from me, unless you have seen our reply to all of your questions and comments personally. And today, I also wanted to answer one of the most common questions. What is an easy way to make money online? Let me solve some of the recent comments that I have received from you. I have taken these screenshots to nicoise asking if I want to earn Khaleb Labasa the same.

I'm a student and I want to make fast money and I don't have any money to start an investment. So in this way, I saw your strategy. How are you going to make money without any investments? And you can start earning like Nicoise, asking then how can I make money using my Android phone even if it's between 400 and one thousand dollars in a month? OK, if you follow this thread you can do it also on your smartphone, also on your Android phone. So follow very closely then.

Besides asking, sir, I need to make more money. So what's Sweden? And I saw you as friends. That will make you more money.

Can I know some apps that earn five or ten dollars per day from playing some games? OK, in this window, I'm not going to show you something that will make you five or ten dollars per day. I'm going to show you that it will make you much more than that, at least one dollar per day. And then Chris was saying great advice. Thank you. I have been looking for ways to make passive income. So in this video, I saw you aware how you can make passive income. In other words, make money while you are sleeping. And then Israel, Ezekial, asks if I want something easy or hard, but it is a technique like clicking to add slowly but easy to make money. OK, so several people have been asking for this easy way to make money.

Now there are, Of course, a lot of different ways to make money online. And if you have been following my YouTube channel, you have seen several different ways to make money from home. Some of them are very easy. Some of them are a little bit harder, maybe. But I wouldn't recommend that you start some easiest way to make money online, because recently I have been doing what is, in my opinion, the easiest way to make money online. That is capture solving. That is so easy that even a five year old person could do it. It's completely so easy. But the problem with that one and also other easiest ways to make money online and they don't pay you, so they really well. So if you are willing to do something that requires some effort, you will usually earn much more money. Then the second point is that anything new is usually hard at first and then it becomes easy.

Think about some of the skills that you have learned during your life, for example, walking or riding a bike, this kind of basic skills or writing or let's say typing on your computer and other normal skills that nowadays you do automatically or for example, using your smartphone nowadays are automatic skills for you. But when you got started, they were hard, but always in life. If you keep on doing more of something, it will become easier and easier and easier and easier. The same is with making money. And if you start today, it may feel a little bit hard for a while, but then it becomes easier and easier and easier for you.

It works in the same way as any other skill. And I would encourage you to think about the reward and the end goal. Like, would you like to make this very easy or easiest money online, which is maybe five dollars per hour with some capital solving? Or would you rather make one dollar a dollar passive income while you are sleeping or laying down a bit or relaxing whatever you want?

Which one do you prefer to think about the end goal? And if you prefer more money in the long run and also making a positive impact on other people, go for the bigger one. Go for the not so easy one. Also, I saw how you can do it quite easily because I believe anybody can do it.

1 Day Work - 9 Days Rest

So my number one recommended way to make money online is affiliate marketing, and if you have seen some of my other videos in the past, you may already know what it means. But if you are new on this channel, I want to explain it to you in a nutshell. Affiliate marketing simply means that you earn money when someone clicks your link and buys some product afterwards. For example, you leave a link to Amazon, somebody clicks it, they go to Amazon, they buy any product on Amazon and you earn money.

Amazon will send you money. And I am also using affiliate marketing to make a living online. And now I'm going to show you five real life examples of companies or products that you can promote. You might copy the link pasted and start making money. And these fire companies. I also promote it myself. So I know that these companies pay real money and I also want to practice what I preach. So I want to recommend the things that I'm using myself that I've seen in practice. These things work so that I can make money. My friends are making money so you can make money.

Also, I don't want to recommend or promote something that I haven't tested or tried myself. So I know and I can guarantee that these companies, these work these pay real money, real costs. So let's dive soon to the screen. And I saw you. And once I have sold you these five real life examples, I'm going to give you two real ideas, step by step ideas, how you can start making money with these five companies. And in the Lincolnesque groups, you can also get started with my one on one support for completely free. The first company that I want to mention is called Let the Market There. And I want to mention this one first, because with them I made my record today, which was three thousand dollars in one day, I believe.

Leave you also a link for that. We are doing the description. So I had me. So you little market, that is a company that provides education and Books and one on one coats and live events for helping people to build their online businesses. And let me see their affiliate programs. So you can see here on the screen there are many different products. So when someone clicks your links and they go, for example, to this page, they fill out their email address and name. They are so called referrals for you. So whatever products they buy afterwards, you earn commissions for that. So somebody may even buy all of these products. And you my own business for that. I have a friend who is part of this alleged market there.

He's one of their affiliates and he started promoting it. And later somebody bought products through his link. And here, like 6000 dollar commissions, like at least three or four or six thousand dollar commissions. And that was like 6000 for sale times for that was like twenty four thousand dollars for forces. That was insane for me because sales are like two thousand dollars. A great thing about the market is that they pay very high commissions, they care for their affiliates and they have very high quality products and live events and all these kinds of things that have a lot of overhead, a lot of profit.

So therefore they can pay a lot of money for people who promote them. And that is the first example. If you want to make one or two dollars per day, let's say you, for example, want to do a lot of comisar. You need to make one sale every ten days for let's say, for example, you make one sale today, the nine days you can rest, then one seven, nine days.

Do the Work Once & Get Paid for Years to Come!

The second product I would mention is called Click Funnel. This is one of the most popular marketing products in the world. There are more than 100,000 users in their Facebook community. There are almost 250000 members on their email list. And in their contact list, there are more than one billion contacts. So it's a huge company making millions of dollars per year. And they provide this software that helps online businesses and all kinds of businesses that will funnel and boost their sales. And they currently have two different main products, click finance and click Finland's platinum and they are 97 dollars per month and 300 dollars per month.

And when somebody buys these through your link, you will earn up to 40 percent commission monthly recurring Comiso. So let's say somebody buys, for example, their basic plan. Through your link, you will earn around 40 dollars every single month as long as they keep staying as a member. And if somebody buys this one, you will earn about one or twenty dollars or something like that. And that is recurring income. So you don't even need to make one sale every day in order to make one dollar per day, because these commissions will start adding up and clicking.

Finance is created by Russell Brunson, who is widely known as one of the best Internet marketers in the whole world. So you can be guaranteed that most likely this company will keep on growing and growing and it's very reliable. Then one of the best programs that I highly recommend that I also promote myself is called wealthy affiliate. This is the community and training. When I originally got started first online, my first online business, I learned the steps on how to make money online. I was a complete beginner myself. I didn't know how to get started, so I simply went through their training. I implemented the steps. I asked the question for the community and that helped me to make a living online. I started traveling around the world and living this laptop's lifestyle.

I achieved much more freedom than I ever dreamed of. They also have this affiliate program and they say here that on average, when somebody clicks through your link and buys something, you earn one hundred twenty one dollars per say. That is the average. For example, my average is much higher than that I have calculated. But there are all kinds of members. So on average, this is one point twenty one dollars per sale. So if you make one sale per day, on average, you will make one hundred twenty one dollars. And they have paid millions and millions and millions of dollars in commissions over the time Book because this company has been around for 15 years.

Let me show you here, as you can see, it's a very reliable website. There have been around since 2000 and five now is 2020. So they have been around for 15 years. One of the oldest companies in the Internet world affiliate threatening. So also wonderful if you are a complete beginner, because as I told you, I got started as a complete beginner without any prior experience and their training helped me to make money online. Now, all these three products, let me show you. Let's affiliate click on us and let the market today be mostly digital products and usually digital products pay high commissions.

As you saw, all of these are like up to 50 percent, even 30 or 60 percent, 20 percent minimum. They are high commissions. And that's why I, for example, promote a lot of digital productivity. How high commissions and also high value. Because let me show you on Amazon, for example, if you would promote something like this, like a piano keyboard or, for example, keyboard for your computer display, lower commission, Amazon pays like three to eight percent commissions. So, for example, if you get five percent commission for this keyboard, you would make only five dollars per sale because this is 100 dollars.

And here you are, five dollars a commission with a piano keyboard. You could earn a little bit more, but if it's five percent commission, you cannot earn so much. And also it would require much more sales to make a full time income. That's why I recommend that if you want to make a full time income, promote digital products.

Practical Examples on How to Do This!

Online Books pay good commissions. Let me give you two examples, so I created this email marketing mastery Book where I teach Step-By-Step how I make money online with email marketing, because most of the income that I have made from the Internet has come through email marketing. So simply writing and sending emails and doing it in an automated way. And in this Book, I teach you the secrets and how I have done it myself and how you can do it. Also, the price of this cause is like four hundred dollars. So if you promote my Book, if you leave a link for this call somewhere and somebody buys through your link, I can pay you 200 dollar commissions. So every time somebody buys my Book through your link, I will pay you two hundred dollars like this. Two out of doors like these, two dollars like this.

Another example of online Books is called Transcribe Anywhere. And I want to mention this because I also promoted this Book. So it's easy for me to talk about it. And I know it's reliable. As you can see, they have different levels and they pay. This pays like 20 percent commission. So it's not as high as on many other online Books. But it's still significant because if you sell, for example, these legal transcripts and Of course, that I have sold also myself, it costs 700 hundred dollars for the customer and 20 percent out of that is around 140 dollars commision. And every time somebody buys, it's what I do for the dollar as well as for the dollar to your bank account or PayPal account.

Now, these are five different products that you can promote and make money online. But now I will give you two real life ideas on how you could make money by promoting these products. So let's have the screen again. Let's take, for example, this transcribe anywhere. So what I did personally, I went to YouTube and I created this transcript anywhere. Review 2020, the best transcription Book online. As you can see here, I will talk about this Book. I tell you why, in my opinion, it is the best transcription Book on the Internet and how it teaches people how to make money online through transcriptions.

So I created this video. I recorded my webcam and uploaded it to YouTube. And nowadays it's there. It's generating views all over the time Book. Then I have a link to risk groups. And so when somebody clicks those links, they go to transcribe any websites. And if they buy some of their Books for some of the products, I earn commissions for that. So that is one idea. You can create a review about that product, Of course, or whatever. You are promoting a record, a review with your smartphone. If your webcam or your camera records a video with your camera, upload that video to YouTube and then leave a link in the description.

Let me know so you can also leave a link in the comments area. And when somebody buys through your link, you will start earning money. And this is completely passive income because I created this video already in the past, but it will keep on generating more income even as time passes by. So that was the first idea. Second idea. Write a blog post. So here you can see a little market review. It's better than ever before here on my blog, your online revenue that comes. We have more than 700 blog posts, Axelle. And one of them is about letting a marketer and here answer all the questions that people may have about the market that I saw as a marketer. Success story is what this little marketer is all about.

I saw inside the members area. I saw how I made three thousand dollars in one day and I told them about their affiliate program. I turned a profit. And Of course, I answer all the questions that people may have. So when somebody pops on Google, for example, lets them market the review, they may end up reading my review and then they get started with a marketer. And when they start, they go through my link and I start earning these commissions potentially if some of them buy these products.

The same with this transcribe and it will review when somebody types transcribe prevue on YouTube. As you can see on the top, there will be my review. So if somebody clicks on what's the story video, they may end up buying the product. So those are two ways you can create a video on YouTube and you can also write articles to your blog.

EASY Ways to Earn Passive Income on This Website

Now you will learn seven ways to make money on Bynum's, you can make money online worldwide, and even for one person free, you can potentially earn a lot of money with these methods. Let's start with the first one, and that is flexible savings. Let's say that you have a hundred dollar bill and you put it under your mattress. Guess how much money you have after one year, you still have the same 100 dollars.

The only thing that has happened is that the value of the bill has gone down during that year. So if you keep your money in the bank account or under your mattress, you will lose money all the time. However, if you hold your money, for example, on buying on the basis of interest, you can make more money simply by holding that money in your account. That is called flexible savings, and I'm using it myself. This works in quite the same way, like local bank accounts that like savings accounts. You submit your money there, you can withdraw it any time you want.

Let's say you submitted it today, you can withdraw it even today, and they will pay you a little bit of interest. However, the difference is that on Bynum's, you can probably earn more interest than in your local bank and in a recent violence, have probably much more reliable than your local bank. Another difference is that you will be submitting crypto currencies instead of government money like the U.S. dollar or euro and so on and so forth. And it's important to point out that with flexible savings, you can withdraw your money any time you want because now we are moving to the number two and that is locked stake. When are you taking on a bonus? You will be saving your money for a certain period of time, for example, seven days or 30 days or 60 days. And neither did you put your money there. Then every single day they will pay you interest.

Let's say you put in the money for 60 days, for example. You lock it for 60 days. They will not pay you money. Only after 60 days will they pay you money every single day as long as your money is locked in there. And then after 60 days, you can withdraw the money and you can do whatever you want with that money. You may be familiar with this kind of investment also in your local bank, like you put your money in for 90 days, then after 90 days, they give you a little bit of interest. However, there are two differences. With bonus, you will probably get higher interest than in your local bank. Second difference is that you get interest every single day, because I remember in my local bank, this is all you get some interest only after this period with bonus, you get interest every day and you're going to immediately start using that interest, not only after 90 days, not only after six days, you can immediately start using it. So in my personal opinion, this is much better than local banks.

And I was positively surprised when I started using this because I saw some cryptocurrency as I have been using this. I'm currently using this because this seems awesome. And I was positively surprised because I thought that I will only get interest after 30 days, after six days. But I started getting interested immediately when I looked at some cryptocurrency.

So it was better than I expected. And the good news is that they are all the time opening up.

New is taking a new look, saving opportunities. There is at the moment, for example, going on this Ethereum 2.0 staking. I will not go into details of that. This would be a topic for a whole nother week. But I'm just mentioning that there are always new opportunities. So I highly recommend you to check it out regularly because there may be even more ways for your money or finance. But let's move right away to the third way.

MORE Ways to Earn Money on This Website

Let's move right away to the third way, and that is a cash back debit card from Bynum's, this gives you up to eight percent cash back. If you're not familiar with cash back before, it means that you buy something somewhere. Let's say you go to your grocery store, you buy something for one hundred dollars and cash back means that you earn some money back for your purchases. If you are, for example, five percent cash back, you get five dollars back out of that 100 dollar purchase. You can order your debit card from Bynum's for 100 percent free. And I have done it recently and I plan to use Pinelands debit card regularly with this card.

By the way, you can buy anything in your local stores simply by using cryptocurrency. So let's say you have Bitcoin or finance going to room or whatever a cryptocurrency on Bynum's. Then you can go to your local supermarket and you can buy food and you can buy anything with those cryptocurrency. So this is also pretty innovative and we are moving immediately into a number four and that is holding cryptocurrency that go up in value. Probably the most common way to make money on buying bonds and also on other cryptocurrency platforms is simply holding your cryptocurrency when they go up in value.

Comparing the US dollars and euros, you earn money, you know, for example, Bitcoin, the value of Bitcoin has consistently been going up, compared to the US dollar and euro, and the chances are that it will keep on going up as the years and decades go on. For example, Bynum's coin is another cryptocurrency before it was worth twenty dollars for one coin. Now it's time to record this video. It's worth over sixty dollars and perhaps even more in the future. But Of course, it's good to keep in mind that the value may also go down compared to the US dollar or euro and other government money.

So you would need to choose carefully with the cryptocurrency you decide to hold. But personally, I will probably hold some bitcoin until the day I die and it's the end of my life because I believe and I see with my own eyes that all the time, more and more people, more and more companies start using Bitcoin. And it's so much easier in many ways than local currency. So I believe in the value of Bitcoin in the long term. So I will be holding that probably for my whole life with a way to earn money. On balance, it's called peer-to-peer trading. With this thirty, you can sell cryptocurrency to other people and provide different payment models because they may be people, for example, who want to buy cryptocurrency using their PayPal accounts. They cannot do it directly from finance because finance doesn't accept PayPal as a payment method. But they provide a platform called peer to peer trading, where people can select crypto currencies and people can buy it using PayPal as a payment method.

So let's say that you hold some Bitcoin, for example, and you want to sell it to somebody who wants to buy Bitcoin and they have a PayPal account. So you can tell them the price and you can make a little bit of profit by doing this kind of trading. They can pay you in PayPal and they can transfer the Bitcoin for them and finance makes the save. So there will not be an excuse if you do this on a bonus. I have also tested this myself. And by the way, I am using six out of the seven strategies to make money on Bynum's.

The only one that I am not using personally myself at the moment is the six one, and that is high risk products. And Bynum's finance provides several high risk products for investing. Personally, I don't have first hand experience of these ones, but not with high risk products. You can potentially earn even more money in a shorter period of time, but you also have higher chances of losing money. So you need to choose carefully. Do you want to earn a lot of money fast, but do you take a higher risk giving it away?

What is the best one for you personally? I prefer to focus on the other six ways to make money on this list, but you can decide for yourself, stick it out always on balance, earn six cents, because as I told you, there is always time for adding new money, making opportunities. So any way to make money on finance is, Of course, the referral program. This is great because you can earn money for a lifetime and even passive income. So you leave a link to the Internet. When people click your link, they sign up to buy us. They start using it. You will be earning passive income for a lifetime.

Apps to Get FREE Bitcoin While You're Sleeping

Recently, I showed you seven apps and websites that make money while you leave my YouTube cameras. I absolutely loved that video and many of you are now earning money while you sleep. However, some of those apps only pay in dollars or in your local currency. Therefore, I want to create a new video that pays you Bitcoin while you sleep.

Once you have earned the three Bitcoins, you can, Of course, exchange them into U.S. dollars or your local currency and use it in your everyday life. Or you can just hold that Bitcoin and expect that the value goes up. There are three criteria when I chose the app to see you in this video. First of all, there must be a mobile app available because I know that many of my subscribers are only using a mobile phone. Second, I have received money from all of these apps, so they are proven to work. And third, they work worldwide because I know that you are from all parts of the world, Africa, Asia, America, Europe. So you can use these apps worldwide to earn money while you sleep.

If you read this video and others saw your three bonus websites, that will also pay you free Bitcoin. Let's start immediately with the first one, and that is that Bynum's balance is the biggest cryptocurrency platform in the world. In one of my recent videos, I showed you seven ways you can earn money on Bynum's. And many of those strategies will make your money while you are sleeping, for example, taking and saving. And I also created the specific we do it when I walked you through click by click how you can earn money by taking and saving finance. So instead of holding your extra cash in your bank account, you can transfer it into Bynum's and it will grow bigger interest and other ways, Of course, by financing affiliate programs that will pay you money for a lifetime as long as somebody clicks your link.

For example, somebody clicked my link over three years ago and I still had like around 100 dollars per week just for that one person who clicked my link three years ago. So that is pretty awesome. Before we move into Blackphone number two, I want to mention that you can get all 10 percent interest on Bynum's through many different ways. You will learn more in my previous videos. But the second platform is called Kukerin and I have been using and also since 2017 as I have used Bynum's as well. It's also one of the biggest cryptocurrency platforms in the universe, and it is estimated that one out of four cryptocurrency holders worldwide is using Kilcoyne. So if there are, for example, 100 million cryptocurrency owners in the world, 25 million of them are using. So it's huge. There are a couple of different ways you can earn money automatically.

Occoquan One of them is, Of course, taking and saving in the same way like in finance. But then there is also cryptocurrency lending. And I have been using this recently because they have all the lending options. And this is pretty interesting. You can lend money to people who need it and then you can earn interest. And at the moment they are paying pretty high interest, as you can see on the screen, and it makes it very safe to lend money to other people, because if somebody wants to lend money from you, they need to have some other assets there. So if they can't pay the loan back, they still have other assets that Kukerin will take from them and they will guarantee the money to you.

And as I mentioned that I'm using the auto lending option. It means that once I lend money to someone and they pay me the whole money and the interest, Kukerin then automatically transfers to the next one and the next one. I always earn interest automatically because that same money will keep on earning the interest because Kilcoyne does all the work for me. Third app is called Celsius Network. On top of that, you will also earn interest on your money. So I just checked it on my phone. I am using it myself as I have been using all of these other platforms as well.

I am earning around five percent interest on my cryptocurrency. So if you have, for example, one thousand dollars worth of Bitcoin, you will earn fifty dollars worth of Bitcoin for free per year. And Of course, when it keeps on growing, you will earn interest on top of your interest. So it will compound over the time Book Celsius network is one of these cryptocurrency savings accounts. So you can keep your money there and you can earn high interest. You can, Of course, hold many different cryptocurrency. Is there at the moment. I have your bitcoin still there and compound and a little bit of Celsius tokens as well, which is their own cryptocurrency Ford platform where you can get free.

MORE Ways to Get Bitcoin Automatically

Platform where you can get free bitcoin is called block free, and this is promoted by numerous cryptocurrency utopias and one of the most famous ones is probably Andre Jike. He has more than one million YouTube subscribers and he offers recommending blog free platforms. Andréa says that you can get up to a 250 dollar bonus when you sign up to a blog for free through his link. However, I signed up using his link and I didn't get a 250 dollar bonus. So I assume that bonus is available only in certain countries and not in my country.

However, it is earning interest for me every single day. So I deposited some Litecoin into a block fee and now I'm earning eight point six percent interest per year on my light coin. So if you hold, for example, one thousand dollars worth of bitcoin there, you will earn eighty six dollars per year interest. If you hold ten thousand dollars, that will be 860 dollar interest per year for the first year. Then Of course, more and more applications are called crypto tabs. And many of you are already earning three bitcoin every single day with this one to be somewhat similar.

Like Hanigan, as many of my users of Scabrous are earning some free money with that. But instead of sharing your Internet connection like you do with Hanigan, you are mining crypto currencies and you will earn free bitcoin for doing that. They also have a nice referral program so you can invite your friends to the tab and then they can also earn money and I suppose you can earn some bonuses for that. Sixth app is called Hanigan. And as you know, I have cashed out hundreds of dollars from Hannegan and my YouTube subscribers have cashed out in total thousands of dollars from Hanigan up. And they pay nowadays also in Bitcoin before they only paid in PayPal. But now you can also cash out the money directly in a Bitcoin account.

It's one of those sets. And forget applications where you will earn a little bit of free money every single day. They also have a daily bonus for active users. So if you are using it with your phone activity in the background, you can log in there once a day and click one button. It's called Ludtke both. You will get a little bit of free money every single day by signing up and clicking that lucky. But it's anything from like a couple of cents to ten dollars per day simply by clicking that button. So that is something to keep in mind. Set app is called The Next, and I love using this. This is another cryptocurrency savings account and it's really easy to use and the interface is really wonderful.

I like it when a user-friendly platform, they pay you anything from five to twelve percent interest on your cryptocurrency and stable coins. It depends on a couple of factors. For example, for cryptocurrency such as Bitcoin and Ethereum, you can earn a five percent interest, however, for stable coins such as US debt. With this data, you can earn even more than 10 percent interest. Then you can earn more if you hold some Nicks opponents with their own cryptocurrency token, and if you take your interest in the form of their own next token, you can earn 12 percent more interest. So it depends a little bit, but the minimum is five percent interest and the maximum is around twelve percent interest per year.

I promise to show you as a bonus, three more apps that you can use to earn free Bitcoin. And these are so-called easy money websites where I will be earning money by reading videos, clicking ads, answering service and doing this kind of other easy tasks. They are called Idle Empire Time Bucks and feature points. I have received money from all of those websites and I have recorded payment proof videos where I saw how I cast money and I show you the proof that they work. These apps are not automatic income apps, but you can also get free bitcoin using your phone because you will need to read videos or click ads or answering service. So it will take a little bit of effort. But there are eight percent free day work worldwide. They work on your mobile phone.

See Step-By-Step How to Earn Money While You Sleep

Step number one, get cryptocurrency, step number two, stake that cryptocurrency, step number three, earn passive income every single day automatically. This is how I am earning money automatically every single day before I see you step by step. How I do it, I must give a legal disclaimer. This is not official investment advice. You take responsibility for your money. I take responsibility for my money. I simply saw in this video how I make money on Bynum's and then you can decide whether you use the same strategy or not. So the first step is to get some cryptocurrency that you can take in order to earn passive income.

And now you're asking how to get cryptocurrency, how to get Bitcoin, Ethereum or some other cryptocurrency that you can take. There are two options. First is that if you already have a cryptocurrency like most other accounts, you can deposit it to Bynum's. I sought to use that process in my previous video where I showed you how I earned six to seven dollars in one hour by reading a video. So you can read that video to learn how to transfer your cryptocurrency to Bynum's second option is that you can buy cryptocurrency online and simply by using your credit card, a bank account.

Now, I will show you how to do that, and you will come to this place that says Create a free account on bindis. Welcome to business. It will put your e-mail address here and your password. Once you have filled out your email and your password, you can simply click here, create an account. But because I have already created an account, I can simply log in here. And I just saw you once. We are in the member area, by the way, if you are wondering what Bynum's is, it's the biggest cryptocurrency bank in the universe. OK, you come inside the members area on bonus and you click here, buy crypto. In the previous video, I explain that you can buy through a bank deposit, credit or debit card.

You can buy even through PayPal, through peer-to-peer trading and also through other payments, like so many payment methods on peer-to-peer trading. But using your card is usually the easiest. So we come here by crypto and then it says the amount you want to buy is. So just for the sake of example, let's buy one hundred fifty dollars worth of cryptocurrency and here you can choose the coin that you want to buy. Now I want to buy A, BNB, which is Bynum's coin because I believe the violence coin will go up in value in the long term.

I'm not going to go into details why I believe Bynum's coin will go up in the future. So now we have put 150 dollars worth of Bynum's coin here and we click here, buy BNB, then we see how much BNB will get and what is the fee in this case? It's only three dollars. And we click confirm and it takes us only a couple of seconds and then we get the balance going immediately. And now within five to ten seconds it is completed.

Check your balance at Voletta so you will see it directly in your wallet. But if you want to earn money by taking, you must come here, click finance and then hereby announce that you earn that amount in different ways. How you can earn money on bonus once you have come here to finance earn six. And there are many different ways you can earn money, such as flexible savings loans, Paul BNB fixed savings, taking activities, and so on. And you hear about the high risk products. These I haven't usually used all of the other ones I have used. I think activities are the only ones that I haven't used for these other ones. In this example, we are talking about staking and we would click here. BNB mordantly stake because we have both been going and then.

Alternative Ways to Earn Passive Income That I Use Myself

And then we could click here stake and then put the max B and B and I have read the agreement and you can read it yourself there. And then you click here, confirm, and then to take the business going and we can start earning free money. And I can show you an example. I have, for example, earned this three point five litten three and let's have a look. What is the price of that? We go to Leeton three ongoing market cap. That is twelve dollars at the moment. And if we calculate with the calculator, I have earned three point five for free and that is ten, twelve dollars.

I have earned more than forty dollars for free by taking finance, going through the little and three cryptocurrency so I can now sell the three bitcoins, a US dollar euro or whatever. And that is just one example of earnings through Bynum's taking. Then we come here to fix the system and we come here taking you to click your view more and Heracles take different crypto currencies. In the previous one, I showed you how to take Bynum's coin, but here you can take other ones.

For example, you can see one in Susi swap Book, polka dot, Cardno, Tomatina, Alexander. So you can see so many different cryptocurrency here. Thrawn, Aeolus Band. You can see dozens of different currencies here and here. You can see the estimate of how much money you will earn, says AP. Why? So this is another person that you are so interested in that you will earn per year. So for example, if you put 1000 Cardno, it estimates around five percent interest. That means you would earn fifty Cordano for free and then you can choose the time that you want to take these, for example, 30 days, 60 days or 90 days. But you can see sometimes it's sold out because so many people are using this, so many people are earning free money with this. And once you have seen that something is available, let me assure you, an example gives here twenty percent interest.

We click the stake now and then you put the amount. How much do you want to take? And once you have read the agreement, then you click here, you can confirm the purchase right here and then it also estimates the interest. So let me show you an example here. You can see if we would take, for example, 50,000 thousand Books, it would give us an estimated interest of more than 440 Books. But Of course, you need to understand that the risk here is that if the value of the specific cryptocurrency goes down compared to the US dollar of Bitcoin, then may lose money. So you need to evaluate. Well, if you want to use that cryptocurrency, if you don't like cryptocurrency, if you want to stay, for example, USDOT, that is the so-called value of US debt, it's always one dollar, so it follows the value of the dollar.

And with this one you can earn around six dollar annualized earnings. So if you put, for example, 1000 USDOT, you would like sixty dollars per year profit with that. At the moment in the current rate you can see the tools here. How long do you want to save it then? It's so for example, like the days you put it here and it will estimate how much interest you will earn. So that is in a nutshell, how you can make money on buying a stake in others. So in a moment, how you can earn even more money with the cryptocurrency saving. So you learn that you can earn six percent profit on your USDOT on Bynum's. But there are platforms that can pay you even more than that. And my recommendation is that you diversify your funds in many different places.

Don't just hold all your money in one bank account, diversify at least two or three bank accounts. So if something happens for a certain bank, you are not at risk of losing money. So I will show you two different places where you're going to stake and save your money so you can earn interest on your crypto currencies. The first place is Celsius network and they give you an interest of twelve point fifty per cent on the USD t and this platform has extremely good reviews. For example, on Trust pilot, there are four points: four stars out of five people absolutely love it because it's giving away free money.

Another platform where you can get similar to sign a bonus. It's called block fee. This gives you a ten dollar bonus when you make your first deposit, then trade worth one hundred dollars and cents to deposit your first money, you can start earning eight point six percent interest on your cryptocurrency investments. So I recommend taking the free money, for example, on Bynum's, but also diversified into a couple of different places. So you diversify your risk.

This WORLDWIDE App Pays You FREE Bitcoin DAILY!

One of the few legitimate cryptocurrency mining apps that pay you real money in this way. I will explain to you how crypto tap works and how you can make money with it, because some of you have been asking me in the comments. Can you tell me about a group for that browser and the best way to earn Bitcoin daily? Because many people have been requesting it today. I will tell you my opinion about it. Let's start by going through their website.

And there are five reasons to use the group the browser earns while surfing the web. So activate the mining, then lead back scrolling news feeds on social media or reading Netflix groups. The tabs will make your money passive income. So it's like making money while sleeping. The fastest build in mining algorithm to one last thing. What I like about the crypto tab is that you can start for free because there have been a lot of cryptocurrency mining scams where they require money from you. But the crypto top you can download for free and start using it. You can use it on your laptop computer or you can use it with your smartphone. So it's also a smartphone application. Then they provide cloud boosts or super boosts where you can earn 10 times more.

And personally, based on my research, I don't recommend this for most people unless you are planning to use this on multiple devices for the long term, because this is like some extra feature. But let's move forward and I will explain to you more about switching to the new browser in a click so you can use this, as I told you, in a smartphone, in a computer, in a laptop, as you wish. You can decide. And some people have been using this on multiple devices. So if you have, let's say for some reason, five or ten smartphones, you can make money with multiple smartphones at the same time, all of them will be making you money. So that's how it works. And so all of your favorite chrome extensions, they have this Krypto tablet like browser.

You can also use it like on Google Chrome. I will show you in a moment, use a group to type on all of your devices. So as I told you, you can use it on all devices. There were five reasons. And then also they explain more here. You can take a look at their website. If you have been looking for the top payment proof. There are many, many, many, many, many on Google. So you can simply type on Google group to type payment proof and you can see dozens, literally dozens of Krypto Tabart payment proof. So based on this information, many people have also been cast out. If you go to YouTube to group the payment proof, you will find many, many, many, many, many, many, many, many of the top payment proofs were people so that they have earned real money. There is also another way of earning money through Krypto Tab, and that is their affiliate program. So let me show you how it works.

You see a real link, for example, of social media or wherever. And then when somebody clicks it and they sign up, you will earn commissions for when they like to start earning money. So let's say that your friend signs up to this website he earns, for example, and they saw you actually on a calculator. He earns ten dollars, you will earn fifteen percent of that. So that will be a one point five dollar bonus for you. Let's say if you have ten friends who do this and all of them are ten dollars, you will earn fifteen dollars. And they also have multiple tyre's here. So if they invite their friends, you will earn a small percentage of that. And if they're friends, so you can earn affiliate commissions into many Tirso that is really nice. And Of course they are providing this as a bonus.

Like if your friend signs up through your LinkedIn, earn the same money anyways, like your commission will be just a bonus. The reason they are providing this is just to incentivize people to share the Descrip tab, because that is how these things grow. That is, for example, how Coinbase, if you have heard of one of the biggest cryptocurrency marketplaces in the world, really exploded thanks to the wonderful referral program. And also you have probably heard that buying Bitcoin access finance actually paid me more than eight hundred dollars in commissions simply by creating a Reavers. When people sign up, they start trading here. I owed more than eight hundred dollars for that. So that's how you use this platform. Scroll through referrals, people recommend them and then some people are earning money by using them.

Some people are earning money as an affiliate. Some people are earning money, for example, in cryptocurrency trading platforms by trading. Some are also losing money and trading. But with a crypto tab, you cannot really lose money. Actually, the only thing you can lose money with is if you go through this, me, you buy these boosts. So with Borst, you can earn, for example, ten times faster. So let's say that normally you would be earning, for example, ten cents per day. Then you bought it ten times. You will be earning one dollar per day. But this is not some new thing that has just popped up. This has been around already for years and tens of thousands, probably hundreds of thousands of people have been.

TRICKS to Earn MORE MONEY with This App!

In this video, I will show you a quick proof of payment and then I will show you a couple of tricks that you can use to increase your earning. These Filipino people here, you can see here earn more than around 1300 dollars from Krypto tab. He started using a couple of tricks of this group. But first, I will show you this. A payment proposal was simply click here, withdraw BTC. OK, then we click here, OK, get it. And then the maximum that we have currently. That is not a lot because we have some time ago cast out, as you saw in my previous video on payment, people have sent us this withdrawal confirmation and we simply need to click this button right here. They say withdrawal confirmed we will make the payment of Bitcoin soon. It will. It takes place within one business day.

In my personal opinion, it's usually been much, much faster. But they probably want to say this so that people will start contacting immediately if it doesn't come in a few seconds. So that's usually pretty fast. So that's how easy it is to withdraw money from group to top. That was just like less than one minute and I already cashed out money from the tab. In a moment, I will show you a couple of the top tricks that you can use to increase your earnings. They have also been on this video where this Filipino person earned around 1300 dollars from the top by mining it. But he has obviously used it more than that. And by the way, if he has kept all this cryptocurrency, the price of that has gone up. And you can see here he had earned around zero point one Bitcoin. And if we put that to BTC, to USD at the moment, that was one zero point one nine. That is more than 4000 dollars USD. So he has earned pretty well from the crypto tab.

And many of my YouTube subscribers have also earned money. You can see here some active miners, they are mining. So it's one of those automatic incomes similar to Hanigan. So simply activated. Whether you are using your smartphone or your computer, you can activate it and start earning a little bit of money. A great thing about this is that you will earn Bitcoin and then you can Bitcoin in the US dollar or euro, unless you have seen the value of bitcoin has gone up and up and up during the last twelve years. So chances are that you will be earning more money, for example, which was cast out a couple of dollars like six dollars. But the chances of that going up is Of course pretty high because Bitcoin has been going up in value all the time.

And Of course, if you want to see more legitimate websites that offer Bitcoin for one percent free to cut my other way to where I saw you, other ones that my subscribers and I have been using to earn Bitcoin for free. But now let's go into those tricks that you can use to earn more money. First, I have to start earning money with crypto. That, Of course, is click here, download. So whether you are using a smartphone or in my case, I'm using an Apple Computer. So I would simply click here, download and then start using it. Second trick is that you start using multiple devices. So let me just Google many smartphones. Many people are using multiple smartphones to make money. You can see you can use as many as you want.

Like if I remember right, there were some people who were using ten smartphones to earn money at the same time on the top. So that will, Of course, increase your earnings because you will have more power over these Filipino people. For example, he was using multiple devices, as he explained in this video. He explained he started two months ago and then he started using many devices and he explains the whole story here. So that's pretty interesting also that the more devices you eat, the more you can earn. You can see the processing here because you can decide where your CPU is. So computing power goes. And here he explains all the details. So I also recommend reading this video.

If you want to increase your earning, then they also provide this cloud boost. With this one, you can earn ten times faster. And at the moment when I'm recording this video, they also have this discount. So be sure to check this out every now and then, because if you buy this boost, it will give you ten times faster earnings. This is especially recommended if you use the tablet multiple devices. If you are using just one device, then it may not be so good. But you can see you can get this cloud that both feeds are up to three devices with the 60 percent discount. So this is crazy and this will give you ten times faster earnings.

I also explained this a little bit in my previous reading, but here are a couple of important facts. It multiplies your speed mining, then it's server dependent mining, no battery drain. So that's also good for your smartphone or your computer. And you can earn unlimited funds. There are no limits on how much you can earn. It's very small, like ten cents or something like that unlimited number of connected remote devices. You can have even ten devices or five devices no matter what. And this is Of course the discount at the moment is just for three devices. But you can connect as many devices as you want and you can also have multiple users.

This is one of the people, Secher, also for public Wi-Fi, and you can earn balance every ten minutes even though you're doing it on autopilot. You simply put the smartphone, stereo, laptop there. It will be earning money every single ten minutes. It. We'll give you and also quick access to the account storing and withdrawing cryptocurrency, as you saw in the beginning, we simply clicked maybe three buttons and then it already came into account.

www.ingramcontent.com/pod-product-compliance
Lightning Source LLC
Chambersburg PA
CBHW071524220526
45472CB00003B/1137